"*Sacred Signposts* is both vinegar and honey to the life of faith—sharply clarifying and deeply fortifying. Benjamin Dueholm writes with the mind of a theologian, the heart of a pastor, and the courage of a prophet—a trustworthy guide to renewed engagement [illegible]

9/18

nd:
e, and Loss

he things
ordinary
derstand

RY

SACRED SIGNPOSTS

Words, Water, and Other Acts of Resistance

Benjamin J. Dueholm

William B. Eerdmans Publishing Company
Grand Rapids, Michigan

Wm. B. Eerdmans Publishing Co.
2140 Oak Industrial Drive N.E., Grand Rapids, Michigan 49505
www.eerdmans.com

Published 2018
Printed in the United States of America

27 26 25 24 23 22 21 20 19 18 1 2 3 4 5 6 7 8 9 10

ISBN 978-0-8028-7417-7

Library of Congress Cataloging-in-Publication Data

Names: Dueholm, Benjamin J., 1979– author.
Title: Sacred signposts : words, water, and other acts of resistance / Benjamin J. Dueholm.
Description: Grand Rapids : Eerdmans Publishing Co., 2018. | Includes bibliographical references.
Identifiers: LCCN 2018001812 | ISBN 9780802874177 (pbk. : alk. paper)
Subjects: LCSH: Christian life. | Spiritual life—Christianity. | Christian art and symbolism. | Sacraments.
Classification: LCC BV4501.3 .D834 2018 | DDC 230—dc23
LC record available at https://lccn.loc.gov/2018001812

This book is dedicated to St. Augustine of Hippo (354–430 AD), who got me into all this trouble, and to Kerry, Soren, Elijah, and Marina, who have helped me get through it.

Contents

Preface

In this book I have varied the language I use for God, who exists beyond all categories, including gender and biological sex. I apply attributes to God by a figure of speech, by an analogy, or just by the cultural idioms human beings inevitably use. When I am closely following the Scriptures, I have preserved the male pronouns for God without capitalization in order to make it somewhat more clear that the male God depicted therein is, in some sense, a literary figure. Similarly, I have preserved the gendered language for God and humanity in the authors I have cited. On some points I may have wished Augustine or Bonhoeffer to have written differently, but I chose to let their words stand as they are.

When speaking apart from particular texts, I have strived to use gender-neutral language. Neither a "traditional" gendered nor an un-gendered discussion of God can avoid the pitfalls of individual and cultural projection, and my particular approach may leave some readers dissatisfied either way. But in the interest of removing potential stumbling-blocks, I offer here my reasoning.

I am a pastor in the Evangelical Lutheran Church in America, serving a local congregation. I trust my debt to my Lutheran heritage will be obvious without seeming like an apology or a polemic. As a pastor, I vowed at my ordination to preach and teach in accordance with the Scriptures, the ecumenical creeds, and the historical Lutheran confessions. The writing of books wasn't specifically addressed in those promises, but I have tried to avoid contradicting these authorities in all that I have written here. Still, if I seem to have failed to represent my faith or my church worthily, the fault is entirely mine. My church, broad and genial though it is, gave me a faithful preparation for my work in ministry and then trusted me to use it well. Neither that church, nor my local bishop, nor my very gracious congregation signed off on anything I have written here. Whatever defects of faith or understanding exist in the pages that follow are my responsibility alone.

Quotes from the Bible are from the New Revised Standard Version, except where, out of habit or aesthetic preference, I have used an older translation, usually the King James.

Quotes from Augustine's *City of God* are from a 1972 paperback edition that, while it has no doubt been surpassed many times over, was my daily companion for two and a half years before and during the writing of this book. I have cited that edition by page number but have also included the book and chapter locations for anyone wishing to look them up in a less antiquated version.

Introduction: The Estate Sale at the End of the World

The practices of a religion are older than the stories we tell to explain them. They engage us more deeply than ideas and more persistently than beliefs. They endure through changes of language and culture, and past the rise and fall of civilizations. They travel, picking up and shedding meanings as they go. They keep parts of us that would otherwise be lost.

Being protean and often shabby, religious practices can easily pass among us unobserved. The candles of a midnight mass may be only a faint memory, but votives flicker in memorial at the site of a prominent death. Household shrines to ancestors may wane, but messages to the departed still appear online and on city streets. There are occasions of sorrow or joy so intense that they call for a hymn, even if that hymn is a treacly secular anthem like "Imagine." We stand for a judge or a national song or a bride. We exercise by twisting ourselves into figures of nature, as if in the presence of a power we've forgotten people once believed in. Believer or not, we take hold of religious practices, and they take hold of us.

If nothing else, a religion is what it does. It is, first and foremost, the space it takes up, the ways it bends its practitioners and their world, the claims it makes on hands and feet, hours and days, effort and attention. A religion's ideas can be argued with, its stories explained away. The practices are mere facts. That is why they may be enacted with such resilience and possessed with such unreasonable fervency. That is why they puzzle and frustrate believer and skeptic alike. That is why they are sacred: they are undeniable.

This is a book about sacred practices in a secular world—what they do and why they matter. More particularly, this is a book about the central, sacred, vexing practices of Christianity, the "holy possessions" by which Christians receive and enact their faith. These practices shape the people who practice them and the world around them. They offer a pointed critique of the unjust and unhappy reality in which they take place, and they offer the outrageous possibility of an alternative. And they do this, as often as not, despite the best efforts of Christians to thwart them.

This is a book about the central, sacred, vexing practices of Christianity, the "holy possessions" by which Christians receive and enact their faith.

As a Lutheran pastor, I am tasked with practicing, treasuring, and handing on these possessions. I struggle with them—with what they do, at the extravagant claims they make, at the complications they impose on my otherwise peaceable existence. That's how I've come to trust that they matter, not just for me and for people who believe and worship much as I do, but for the whole world, too. They don't need anyone's belief or doubt; they keep happening through both.

In the part of the world that considers itself secular, where religious identification and participation are in crisis, our practices preserve and embody faith in a way that no polemic or apology can. And at the same time, those practices address themselves to a world that, however secular or advanced, is experiencing its own crisis, an intense intimation of its own mortality. These Christian practices represent and enact a different vision of what it means to be good, or even to be human, from the ones offered by our prominent political and economic ideologies. Christians have names for this different vision. We call it "the kingdom of God" or "the beloved community." And it is realized, in ways that are small and fleeting but also urgent and poignant, every time we gather around our holy possessions.

So before we grasp the possessions themselves, I want to say a little about how they, and we, arrived at this particular moment.

◈ ◈ ◈

Once upon a time there was something called Christendom. An irregular and happenstance mingling of a Jewish end-times movement, Greek philosophy, and the administrative apparatus of the Roman Empire, Christendom lived for centuries over vast stretches of the globe. It birthed experiments in living, institutions of learning, varieties of worship, objects of devotion, systems of thought, social ethics, and radical movements. It abolished some of the evils of the pagan world it conquered, refurbished others, and invented some of its own. It hooped churches and states and cultures together in an ever-shifting but seemingly unbreakable bond, despite schisms and reforms, civil wars and revolutions. Christendom touched everything in its domain. Even dissent, even atheism—such as it was—borrowed its dress, its habits, and its obsessions.

Then it fell ill and died. The illness was mysterious, a gathering of a thousand pathologies within and without, palpable and hidden. The terminal diagnosis may have been made as early as 1789, when the Old Regime fell in France, or as late as 1859, when *The Origin of Species* began to move the human story beyond the claims of sacred and philosophical texts. The patient was gone by 1945, after Christian Europe expended its last heroic fury in destroying its institutions and, not coincidentally, the very people from whom its central figure comes.

When the pulse finally stopped, a terrifying liberation followed. Churches were disambiguated from governments and cultures, only to discover just how much they had depended on both for their identity, for the meaning of all the things they taught, practiced, and cherished.

There was still growth and dynamism—Christendom's hair and nails, so to say—as churches reexamined their thought and practice in light of catastrophes they had been, at best, powerless to stop. Some churches dramatically revised their relationship with

Jews and Judaism, recognizing too late the poison enclosed in their anti-Jewish doctrines. Liberation movements in the colonies of Christendom forced churches to rethink the identification of their faith with "the West" or "Europe." Liberation movements at home forced them to redefine the societies they claimed to teach and protect—whether by including the oppressed or excluding them more strictly. Experiments in theology and liturgy, both noble and foolish, undertook to reignite the spark in the stiffening body.

The United States, less ravaged by 1945 than her European cousins, stood as an impressive exception. For two more decades the churches kept growing and expanding, generating and absorbing revival movements and media celebrities, academic innovations and populist nostalgia, political argument and social upheaval. But the bell rang out eventually here, too. The world after Christendom—which some simply call "post-Christian"—arrived.

America, too, is experiencing a significant, ongoing decline in formal religious participation and identification. Immigration has bolstered some religious communities. But among people born in the United States, religion in general and Christianity in particular are in significant retreat. Catholic and historic Protestant parishes shrink and close in their traditional heartlands. Evangelical megachurches struggle to hold worshipers after their charismatic founders leave the scene. Church construction has fallen to its lowest rate in many decades. There are fewer adherents, and those who remain participate less regularly. The every-Sunday stalwarts of the mid-century are dying and being replaced, if at all, by smaller families who give their time to work, social activities, or simply the scramble that attends increasing economic insecurity.

Religious ideas have lost their role in explaining the world. Evolutionary biology has kicked God out of the chain of causes that led to life as we know it, economic and political theories did the same for society, and now psychology and neuroscience have prized open the doors behind which we locked God after he absconded from the causes of the visible world. The Christian story is no longer the primal story from which all others spring; now it is a development in some other primal story told by evolutionary or cultural or economic theory. The Christ who stood before and outside history, spanning parliament house and church altar and heaven, became the "historical Jesus," a man defined by his time and place.

These secularizing developments contradict each other. Sometimes they contradict themselves. But they've changed the terrain on which we experience and argue over faith. They are not new or unprecedented; they are not the result of intrinsic progress. Our secular, modern age has its own intellectual conventions and taboos, its own invisible influences and forces. Our age is just another turn of time's wheel.

But we turn with it. Modern-day believers can easily feel alienated or even threatened by this moment. Our history did not prepare us for it. It's not that religion has exactly disappeared. City streets and social media feeds overflow for a charismatic pope; religious groups can be mobilized as decisive voting blocs; new religious identities crop up between orthodoxy and atheism; exotic ritual and spiritual practices gain cachet, all while the communion line dwindles, the parish ebbs away, and the bonds of religious life fray beyond recognition.

This, for Christians, is the world after Christendom. Like anyone else, we are responding to a death in the family with a familiar mixture of heroism and neurosis. Since Christendom died without leaving a will, every conflict among Christians over doctrine, politics, worship, and morals has been part of a massive, decades-long, globe-spanning estate sale among fractious heirs. Some of us haven't spoken in a long time, some of us have only been getting reacquainted since the funeral, and most of us disapprove of each other in some degree.

We divide ourselves by theology, politics, geography, and language. But cutting across those more obvious distinctions is a divide in how we are managing the estate. Some of us are historic preservationists. These haven't quite given up on recapturing the heart of American or Western civilization for Christianity. They treasure the great philosophies and theologies that anchored Christendom, the structures of authority and discipline, the thick and coherent traditions. They strive to recreate the old Christian household in diminished terms, safe from the rumblings of the modern world and ready to reclaim the town square when that world collapses under its own contradictions. Others of us, however, are dumpster-divers. They aren't dreaming of any return or revival of Christendom, which they view as a fundamentally corrupt bargain between church and state. Instead, they are busy scavenging and repurposing the items they value from the estate of Christendom—the immediate spiritual experience, the radical egalitarianism, the eclectic practices and local truths—for use in a post-Christian, post-religious world.

I've done my share of both historic preservation and dumpster diving. Both are compelling and both cause problems. Historic preservationism can make people authoritarian, reactionary, and defensive. Dumpster diving can make us diffuse and marginal, light in commitment and ready to claim any enthusiasm in the world for Christ.

But if, instead, we renew our focus on those Christian possessions shared by all, perhaps we can understand both our faith and each other better. If we turn away from an ideal Christianity to be preserved from the past or built in the future, perhaps we can see better what Christians already do and already are. Because despite our apparent marginalization, our differences and manifest failures, what happens among Christians can still astonish.

And it needs to. Because outside of our family estate sale, the secular, modern world after Christendom is receiving its own frightening diagnosis. Brilliant and powerful as we may be, we are just waking up to the harsh reality of our own limits. Our political institutions and cultural norms can't protect us from ourselves, our ecological footprint is not compatible with a recognizable future, and our technology nears the point where it can absorb and abolish us. The Yellowstone Supervolcano is also overdue, in case you were wondering. And we could do everything right and catch every break and still wander into a deep-space object or a bursting cosmic bubble. We've outlived all our optimistic scenarios, not excluding the terrifying but comparatively sensible scenes of the Last Judgment on the canvases and altars of Christendom. The universe will give us and everything else an end as undignified and meaningless as it is inevitable.

So it happens that those who cling to the practices of faith inhabit a double fragility and experience a double anxiety: first, as outliers in a world that doesn't need, and even seems hostile to, religion; second, as citizens of that world that feels and fears its own mortality. Grasping our holy possessions more faithfully and passionately won't help us deny or evade that fragility and anxiety, and it won't heal our internal divisions. But grasping our holy possessions can turn us outward, to a world that needs a kind of healing it can neither imagine nor grant. Grasping our holy possessions can't fix the world—it would have by now if it could—but it can resist this world and point to another one.

Grasping our holy possessions more faithfully and passionately won't help us deny or evade that fragility and anxiety, and it won't heal our internal divisions. But grasping our holy possessions can turn us outward, to a world that needs a kind of healing it can neither imagine nor grant.

These possessions can even make that other world real, in a limited way, in little patches of space and time. They offer a kind of freedom and an experience of solidarity and an expression of hope that none of our pinched and gloomy ideologies can explain, much less offer. And they do this because they are not other-worldly or even "spiritual" at all, but because they are brutally worldly and literal. They are not ideals, but real things that anyone can take hold of, and that can change anyone who does.

◈ ◈ ◈

In speaking of "holy possessions," I am following the terms and inventory of the Christian household made by the sixteenth-century German church reformer Martin Luther. This is not because Luther was right about everything, or anything in particular, but because his age had a strange affinity with ours. Luther's age had its own budding secularity, its own new freedom from religious limitations, and its own bloody and tragic estate sale as Christendom and its effects were divided between hostile camps.

When he was forced to answer the question of how to identify the church of Jesus Christ—or, as he called it, "the holy Christian people"—Luther chose to focus on these possessions, items in our common inheritance so important that we've argued about them ever since:

> words, which confront the people who hear or read them with startling demands and promises, stories that provoke

faith and court disbelief, and ethical quandaries that challenge the most virtuous person (Luther called this "the holy Word of God");

water, through which people receive a new identity and a new relationship with God and each other ("the holy sacrament of baptism");

a meal of bread and wine which become the body and blood of Christ, celebrating union and creating solidarity among people the world prefers to separate ("the holy sacrament of the altar");

confession and forgiveness, which offer and give ludicrous pardon and release from all sins and the world's brokenness ("the office of the keys");

ministry, which sets embarrassingly ordinary people apart to celebrate these holy possessions on behalf of the whole community;

prayer, praise, and worship, which steal time and labor away from the world to allow another kind of life to be known;

the cross and suffering, which compel Christians to identify with the oppressed and exploited.

These possessions are a place to start, rather than to end. They are guides, signposts marking out an unlikely itinerary into attention, consideration, and even to faith. They indicate the limits of the religious and secular ideologies of our own time. And they direct us to the possibilities of both past and future, both within and beyond ourselves.

This book comes out of years of repeating, revising, and sometimes rejecting the arguments of Martin Luther and many other Christian thinkers. It springs from my attempts to preserve, or else salvage, my own best picture of Christian faith and life. I became a Christian while a student at the University of Chicago at the turn of the century. I was chasing God in those days, tracking his footprints around corners, in books and poems, through dreams and visions. Then, in an instant, I ran into something solid—a cross traced in ash on my forehead—and fell over, skidding to an embarrassing slapstick repose.

A few years later and three miles west, in Englewood, my faith was taken apart at a little church that stood between a blank field and a neighborhood hollowed out by redlining and the retreat of the state. The word, the bathing, the meal, the forgiving of sins, the role of the leader, the worship were all there. So was the suffering, which to me was new, and which changed the meaning of every other possession of God's people. I was given a new picture of what my faith could be and mean, and it is one I have seen and elaborated over and over again, over these possessions shared and celebrated at the broken edges of the world, among people, like me, traveling in a retrograde motion against the background of a cosmos turning to empty itself of God. There, and ever since, Christianity did not appear as a shelter from the world's storm, but as the ship in the storm's midst; not a dialogue in which a private truth could be seized, but a proclamation to the whole world; not an accessory to our politics and our ideologies but a blatant and scandalous judgment on both. It is not an explanation of the world, but the thing that resists explanation. It is not an interpretation of the world, but the thing that demands interpretation. It is not the thing that is challenged by the secular reality around me. It is the challenge.

And that challenge is where we begin.

Chapter 1

WORDS

The Archive of the Inconsequential

And on the day called Sunday, all who live in cities or in the country gather together to one place, and the memoirs of the apostles or the writings of the prophets are read, as long as time permits; then, when the reader has ceased, the president verbally instructs, and exhorts to the imitation of these good things.

—Justin Martyr,
First Apology, chapter 67

The Economy of Giving a Damn

Life is an endless war of all against all for our attention. Each moment, each choice, each thing we encounter poses us a question: Do I matter? We use our words and conversations, assembling them into great discourses and worldviews, to answer that question. From the earliest Greek philosophers to Google's search algorithm, we've been trying to decide how to ration our scarce attention and concern. We list our priorities. We decide if something is important in itself or for some other purpose. We create an economy of giving a damn.

And into that economy of giving a damn, the first holy possession introduces serious instability. Every day, in almost every language, Christians open up this first holy possession, the Word of God. It comes to them on the printed page, in spoken sermons, in chanted hymns.[1]

That Word, like all other conversations and discourses, is about deciding what matters. It shows forth a world created by God and continually mended and redeemed by God. It confronts those who hear it with infinite demands and infinite possibilities. It challenges their values and scrutinizes their choices. Most importantly, it upends their assumptions about whose existence matters and requires attention and respect.

Some Christian societies have testified to the holiness and the danger of this Word by prohibiting it in various forms. Owning the Scriptures in translation was, once, a political crime. An antebellum politician in South Carolina, arguing successfully to prohibit teaching slaves to read and write, insisted that anyone who wanted slaves to read the whole Bible belonged "in the Lunatic Asylum."[2] The powerful, wishing to be free to use the poor and lowly, did not want those poor and lowly to hear that God had not made them to be used. And those poor and lowly, when they heard those words, kept and treasured them, and resisted oppression by them.

It is hard to imagine everything mattering as much as the Word tells us it does. It is much easier to ration significance, to focus on the big picture. As a preacher, I am aware of techniques we use to blunt the confrontation, to impose some stability on the economy of care and concern that is threatened by the Word.

We confine it to metaphor or symbol, or to an irrelevant past, or to the overzealousness or exaggeration of a biblical author. We rebrand it as a source of life principles for getting ahead or being proper. Søren Kierkegaard, the Danish theologian and philosopher, compared these techniques to bargaining down the price of merchandise.[3] The Word becomes an item for sale in a skeptical market.

But this possession, like all those that follow, doesn't sit on the shelf awaiting a buyer. The Word acts on those who hear it. It leaves an impression of what we would otherwise forget or discard. It guides and directs us to possibilities, both dreadful and hopeful, that we might otherwise have no way to see. And to do this, it does not require our faith, but only our curiosity. It does not require conviction, but openness to other ways of seeing and thinking. It marks out the frontier of a very different economy of concern than we would otherwise know, and invites us to enter.

The Word acts on those who hear it. It leaves an impression of what we would otherwise forget or discard. It guides and directs us to possibilities, both dreadful and hopeful, that we might otherwise have no way to see. And to do this, it does not require our faith, but only our curiosity. It does not require conviction, but openness to other ways of seeing and thinking.

Do I Matter? A Case Study

On a day-off ramble not long ago, my son Elijah and I found a newborn mouse stranded on a white-painted stripe in the church parking lot. It was tiny, eyes still covered and unable to walk. It hurled itself vigorously one way and another, far from any hospitable place. One of the neighborhood hawks must have let it slip.

A miserable, orphaned creature, once seen, cannot be unseen. Its fate instantly implicated us. I'm not tender-hearted toward mice. In California, where they carry Hantavirus, I killed them without pity by water trap and boot heel. Nonetheless, there is solidarity in mammalhood. If we watch a fellow creature strive blindly toward a mother it will never find, we should not be unmoved.

Elijah, only two, would have taken the wrong lesson from a mercy killing. So we moved the mouse pup, carefully, in a Styrofoam cup, and bedded it in the deep, cool grass along a fence behind the parsonage. We gave it some milk from a dropper. Its jaws gaped and its mouth shuddered. Then down the fence it lunged in its blind search.

"Mouse," Elijah said, matter-of-factly. He was old enough to find it interesting but still young enough to be immune to its pathos. It was just a thing he had a word for, distinct from the grass, the fence, his dad.

Later on, I returned to check on our unhappy friend. It was nowhere to be seen. When I turned toward the front yard to meet our older son's school bus, he ran out to me, crying. "I thought you were missing or dead," he told me, through unfeigned tears. (We'd just read a book by Roald Dahl, poet laureate of the orphaned boy.) His worry at finding the house empty was appropriately excessive for a child. But his intuition—that life is a hawk with an uncertain grasp—was perfectly correct.

Did the mouse matter? Was it good or wise to spare even as much time and thought as we did to soften its end? Untold ancestors had scrambled to assemble the DNA that wove that mouse. Their momentary dumb lives had issued in that marvel of engineering—muscles, nerves, filigreed bones bending ferociously toward survival. But it failed. No sooner did it wake to the world than it slept with its fathers, a dead end in a trivial suburb of evolutionary history.

Augustine, the late fourth-/early fifth-century bishop, called the multitude of short-lived creatures on the earth "castaways," little things "doomed so swiftly to perish."[4] A random world full of ephemeral, suffering things may reveal, as Augustine believed, the great care and ingenuity of God. But it also demands choices and trade-offs. And we have developed very useful ways to make those choices. A dying mouse pup is meaningless to evolution, because it leaves no issue. It was not useful to anyone or productive of any value, according to economics. It had no status in the human community. Any attention it received was wasted.

Our leading ideas and influential worldviews are about the big picture: the arc of history, the Darwinian winners who secure their posterity, or waves of innovation that bring progress and prosperity for as many as possible. We have good reasons not to busy ourselves with an orphaned mouse pup lost in the ticking gears of the cosmos. We have taught ourselves to focus on the big stuff.

But what if every insignificant and suffering thing expands like a fractal to the shape of the universe? What if it's all big stuff? And if it's all big stuff, how do we make choices and live our lives? That is the startling, poetic, impossible challenge issuing from this Word that is the first essential holy possession of Christians.

What if every insignificant and suffering thing expands like a fractal to the shape of the universe? What if it's all big stuff?

The Unmuzzled Ox and the Fallen Sparrow

When Christians gather for worship, they gather around a vast and unruly archive of words: ancient stories preserved from oral traditions, prophetic utterances, chronicles of kings and queens, wars and migrations, poetic dialogues, and moral and legal precepts. We call this anthology the Scriptures. They illuminate and teach. They also mystify and perplex. They scatter oddities and outliers—words and ideas orphaned by the sweep of great stories and the march of the ages.

A person who encounters the Scriptures today, whether as a divinely inspired "Holy Bible" or merely a collection of ancient literature, can scarcely help but find them old and strange. Their calm or even celebratory accounts of monstrous crimes, their implausible miracles, their ethical and historical contradictions—all of these have inspired criticism since ancient times.

But much of the distance between the Scriptures and the modern readers who hear and digest their thorny words comes from the claims those words make about what requires and deserves our care and attention. For a book filled with so much pain, the Bible makes pain into a problem. This heap of words covering centuries and great nations draws our attention to the world's castaways.

The difficulty starts in the beginning. God says, "Let there be light," and so at a word the universe is up and running. In swift succession all else follows, from the heavens and the waters and the land, to the swarm of fish and crawling things, to male and female humans created in God's image. Finally, God creates rest.

The Word of God has always been one among many words, one story among many others trying to make sense of the world and of human life. To create the universe through speech was an odd choice. The other gods of the ancient Near East didn't do it that way. They brought the world into existence through violence or sex, not through words. The account of the biblical book of Genesis almost seems designed to contrast with the creation stories of Babylonian religion. In those stories, the world is fashioned from the corpses of slain gods, and humans are created to feed the victors with their sacrifices. This God, the story seems to be saying to its audience, is different. This God creates with speech, not violence; this God created you in God's own image, and the world for your nourishment. This God ordains your rest, not your unending labor.

So when we encounter this Word today, no less than when it was first written down, we encounter an offense. We hear that the world, in the grandeur of its entirety and in the democracy of its detail, was made as an act of pure, free, non-violent speech. But everywhere else we hear political myths and cultural stories about competition and destruction. We hear that the world was made in peace, yet we see it everywhere at war. We hear that humanity is made in the image of God, and yet we see that image everywhere enslaved. We hear that God rests and commands rest, yet all things are full of labor. We hear that God looked on everything he had made and saw that it was good, yet we see this goodness divvied up, parceled out, and squandered by conquest and commerce.

From the start, the Word insists to those who hear it that the world was not always—and need not always be—as it is now.

These words of God continue through the stories that follow, lifting up the obscure and insignificant, and displacing the great and mighty. God calls a people—not, he points out, a numerous people, but rather the smallest of peoples. God takes their side against a mighty, civilized kingdom. And God speaks to them in laws that direct the concern of those who hear them. Debts must be forgiven. Slavery must not be perpetual, and freed slaves must be given resources for freedom. A widow's cloak must not be taken as a pledge for a debt. The windfall of the orchard and the margin of the field must be left for orphans, widows, and foreigners who have no land to raise their own crops. One whole day must be set apart for rest, and on that day no one—slaves, servants, children, citizen or foreigner—may work.

The Sabbath command extended even to animals. Even the ox that is treading out your grain must not be muzzled while it works, so that it can eat as it goes, the Law says. That farm animals need rest and food in order to be useful is obvious. No regulation on the matter is needed. But the Law goes beyond mere necessity: it enjoins rest to the animals for their own sake, and forbids the routine cruelty of preventing them from grazing on the food they produce.

Does the farm animal matter? The Word answers that it does. Its life comes from God. It is an end in itself. So much more is the widow and the garment that keeps her warm, the landless person and the food she gleans, the laborer and the rest that restores her body and soul. The Word addresses itself to these and the margin on which they survive. It makes the life of each worthy of respect and kindness regardless of the cost we must bear to extend that respect and kindness to each other.

But this answer—yes, they all matter, even the farm animal—has continually provoked rejection and disbelief. For the wise and sophisticated, all of these exist to be used. Relief from debt, rest from labor, fields for gleaning are all so much loss and inefficiency. Seneca, the great Roman philosopher and dramatist, found it outrageous that Jews "practically lose a seventh part of their life in inactivity."[5] The waste imposed by God is an evergreen complaint. Wasted time, wasted effort, wasted wealth—all lavished on the ungrateful, unworthy, and unnecessary in the world.

The waste imposed by God is an evergreen complaint. Wasted time, wasted effort, wasted wealth—all lavished on the ungrateful, unworthy, and unnecessary in the world.

So it happened that the utterances of God did not conclude with the laws given to God's people. The Word continued in prophecy to confront gods and ideologies that sought to silence the peculiar, disruptive view of life expressed in those cumbersome rules about days of rest, widows, oxen, and farm fields. The Word spoken by the prophets vigorously and creatively applied those laws to the changing circumstances of God's people.

When we hear the Word in prophecy, we hear of a day when the words of God reach the ends of the earth and restore the nations to peace and unity under the rule of God. We hear about the child playing over the hole of the asp, the wolf and the lamb lying down together. It can seem quaint, this vision of wholeness. We hear of conquering armies turned back and swords beaten into plowshares. We hear a promise that God will wipe away the tears from each face. All flesh—even the mouse straining hopelessly toward its mother—will see God, who saves both humans and beasts.

In these words of hope and expectation, we hear that the big picture is not the dominion of one empire over another, or the rule of one favored class or nation, but of a world put back together, as it was created, by words. The multitude of dead and failed and lost will all be vindicated at last.

Then we hear Jesus. Speaking from the engraved stone of Law and the fire of Prophecy, he brings the flagrant excess of care and concern dispersed throughout the Scriptures to a dramatic pitch. The words of the Law and the Prophets cause our economy of giving a damn to tremble. The words of Jesus raze it to the ground.

Many Christians, in a pious gesture, stand up when the stories of Jesus are read in church. Within the holy possession of the Word, the words spoken by and about Jesus are treated as particularly holy. But it might be more appropriate to take shelter.

> Then we hear Jesus. Speaking from the engraved stone of Law and the fire of Prophecy, his words bring the flagrant excess of care and concern dispersed throughout the Scriptures to a dramatic pitch.

Jesus speaks about the birds of the air not sowing or reaping, yet filled by God, and the lilies of the field not toiling or spinning, here today and gone tomorrow, yet clothed in greater glory than King Solomon. And Jesus tells his hearers to learn from the flowers and the birds. He speaks of jots and tittles and calligraphic flourishes that will be held and preserved past the end of time. We hear him say that ordinary folk are the salt that seasons the earth, the light that fills the world, and the yeast that leavens the whole batch of dough. We hear him welcome children, when brutes treated them as fair game for massacres and the civilized exposed them in trash heaps. We hear him insist that God's kingdom belongs only to those who become like those defenseless children.

We hear his warnings, too. If our eyes cause us to stumble, he says, we must pluck them out. It's better to lose a part of ourselves and enter life than be cast into hell. If our thoughts tend toward adultery or murder, he warns us, we're already guilty of it. If we neglect the least of his own who are naked, hungry, or incarcerated, we neglect Jesus, and we will rue it forever. He says all these things from the midst of his odd clique of fishermen, teachers, prostitutes, and rich kids on a lark.

We stand up to be told these things. We stand up to be confronted in this way, to be challenged in the poverty of our concern, the shortness of our vision, the wretched efficiency of our giving a damn. We hear, in these words, not just the Law and the Prophets already spoken to daily needs and long-run hopes. We hear those needs and hopes intensified. We hear of a Kingdom of God foretold and expected to come, but already present by faith and love.

In the microcosm of his community of disciples, the words of Jesus reveal an eternal *now* in which the human and the sparrow alike eat their fill, and lily and human are together arrayed in unfading glory. We are told to value radical generosity over wealth, spiritual poverty over visible righteousness, daily bread and the Kingdom of God over tomorrow and its needs. Christians sometimes claim, doubtfully, that Jesus was executed because of his words. Pontius Pilate, grim administrator of the Roman order, did not likely care about the lilies and the sparrows and the prostitutes. But he imposed crucifixion, a punishment so cruel and public that only non-citizens could receive it, in a bloody coda to those words. We hear, in that story, all the lost things and lost causes of the Scriptures and the world, the mouse pups and sparrows and widows and orphans summed up in one forsaken voice. We stand up, at last, to be overwhelmed.

Deflection

This holy possession—this archive of the inconsequential—inevitably provokes opposition. Not least from Christians. We hear these words, read these stories, chant these poems, and then must find a way to toggle back to the world we know. And here, outside that Word, the other words and other gods remain ready to persuade us that what matters *there* need not matter so terribly much *here*.

Surely, Christians have held, God did not intend to impose all these flagrant inefficiencies on the employer, landowner, or creditor. When the United States practiced slavery, the slaves could be muzzled in the fields and denied a Sabbath. When, by force of arms, slavery was abolished, the slaves could be freed without provision for their independence. We make much of the harshness of the Scriptures, but our own laws long were, and in some ways still are, much harsher.

And anyway, do our thoughts and intentions really matter so much as we hear Jesus say? We must deserve some credit for stopping between the thought and the adultery, between speaking a word in rage and landing a deadly blow.

Christian or not, people are good at deflecting the confrontation of the Word. The laws of the Old Testament are old and weird. Or, as Christians have said, they are abolished by Christ, leaving us free to practice slavery and debt servitude as we think will be most beneficial. The diamond-hard commands of Jesus are not binding on us, but "counsels of perfection" for religious specialists. Or else they are there only to show us how sinful we are, and how badly we need God's grace and forgiveness.

We erect barriers between people who are merely curious and the Word itself. To approach this holy possession, you may first be asked to adopt a certain view of what it is.

For fundamentalists, this barrier may mean accepting the text as literally true in a very modern way, reducing all knowledge to mere information. To understand the Scriptures, then, means first believing they are true in one particular sense, as a glorified textbook or user's manual.

For other Christians, influenced by modern "critical" methods of study, this Word may be called a product of the culture and ideologies of the societies that produced it. Pruned away are difficult or implausible passages, and our own views are confirmed by what is left.

These chivalric efforts on behalf of the Word are meant to keep it plausible and "relevant" to believer and doubter alike. Fundamentalists defend the text by waving off even well-founded questions. And by refining poetry, legend, and allegory out of the holy possession and pounding it flat, they reveal the shape of the anvil underneath—the social agendas or "life principles" the Word now serves. Likewise, the critics diminish the stark challenges of the Word and give us Paul, the neurotic, self-hating Jew, or Jesus, the peasant philosopher whose needy followers blew him out of proportion.

Either way, we are given not a holy possession but an echo of the cacophony of the world we already have—richer in knowledge than imagination, greater in confidence than consensus. We package the Word, like everything else, for sale and lose the ability to hear it on its own terms and in its own voice.

This bargaining isn't necessary. The Word of God still attracts, repels, puzzles, and illumines those who hear it with a heart even slightly ajar. It needs no defense and no plausible branding. Whether each word was penned directly by God, or it's just a bunch of stories told by herders and religious enthusiasts around campfires, the Word simply *is*, for the one who hears it and dares to envision the vistas it opens.

When Martin Luther identified the Word of God as "the principal item, and the holiest of holy possessions," he wasn't writing as our modern fundamentalists or critics do.[6] He meant that the Word was an active and living force. It was not given to us to be an object, even an object of belief. It wasn't even primarily a written text, but first and foremost a spoken proclamation. It was given to reveal God. For Luther, and hardly him alone, the Word was a subject. It accomplished things.

When Luther opened this holy possession, he witnessed two things: God giving infinite commands, and God making unqualified promises. The commands provoked the fear of judgment. The promises invited trust and gave assurance.

Luther's intense focus on commands and promises does not exhaust the meaning of the Word. But his essential insight was sound. This possession provokes the one who hears it, changes the one who hears it, redirects the one who hears it. Through that hearer, it can change the world. Both the commands and the promises—and everything else—insist to skeptical believers and curious doubters alike that they, their neighbor, and all of life are infinitely significant.

That infinity of significance is the great blessing and heavy burden of this peculiar holy possession. More than the outlandish stories, more than the horrible crimes, the infinity of significance draws the line between the temptation to believe and the urge to doubt.

The Weight of Perfection

At a turning point in his ministry, Jesus warns a wavering would-be disciple, "No one who puts a hand to the plough and looks back is fit for the kingdom of God." It is, as Jesus's followers sometimes said, a hard saying. Who can bear it?

I say these words. I expound them to rooms full of Christians. They are attentive, sullen, distracted, searching, and all of them, like me, are divided in heart and work and concern. We are together the heirs of traditions that have treasured the sharp commands to free the captive and welcome the stranger and that have found ways to avoid those commands. Does a backward glance from the plough matter so terribly much? If there is any group of Christians so single-minded as to have never second-guessed, to have never indulged in a wistful glance toward another road, I am not among them.

The mouse's path and ours, after all, diverged quickly. If I had any obligations to it, as God's people have to the beasts of the field, and as God feeds the birds of the air, I did not fulfill them. For a month or two, Elijah would point to the place we'd left it. "Mouse gone." The Word proposes a weight of perfection that no life can bear.

It is the moment of confrontation with the Word, the eternal *now*, that bears that weight in its infinite significance and untamed possibility. In Jesus's story, the "Good Samaritan" crosses a dangerous road to tend to a bleeding man. He doesn't risk his life for a stranger as a step on the road to perfection. He does it as if it were the only decision in his life that would ever matter.

It is the moment of confrontation with the Word, the eternal *now*, that bears that weight in its infinite significance and untamed possibility.

As long as the Word is at hand, and someone is there to hear it, the confrontation can happen. That infinity can break into the compromised moment in which every hearer of the Word lives. A community can form around that confrontation. Every tawdry and foolish hierarchy, every system of exploitation and cruelty, every mad design to escape or limit the scope of our humanity has been confronted by the Word—ours included.

To those who hear it, the Word reveals the Kingdom of God as an empire of attentiveness, a radically different economy of giving a damn that subverts our world's rationing of significance. It records what we can only forget, stores up what we can only lose, sets free what can profitably be kept in bondage. When it confronts us, with all its glories and gargoyles, it beckons us to participate in that economy, if only for a moment or a day at a time.

The Word prepares us for the work of all the holy possessions that follow. It is the point of departure, and the continual guide, for the itinerary these signposts mark out for us. Like the Word, they will make the distant draw near. They cast down the mighty and lift up the lowly. They give us what is strange and cast out from us what we know. And like the Word, all the holy possessions that follow do not demand belief or spurn doubt, but open a space of possibility between them, simply by being experienced. The first and principal holy possession calls together a people to cherish and embody it, who are willing to see its dramatic possibilities made real among them. Those possibilities take shape in the initiation of Christians through baptism.

Chapter 2

WATER

Insiders and Outsiders

At cockcrow prayer shall be made over the water. The stream shall flow through the baptismal tank or pour into it from above when there is no scarcity of water; but if there is a scarcity, whether constant or sudden, then use whatever water you can find. They shall remove their clothing. And first baptize the little ones; if they can speak for themselves, they shall do so; if not, their parents or other relatives shall speak for them. Then baptize the men, and last of all the women; they must first loosen their hair and put aside any gold or silver ornaments that they were wearing: let no one take any alien thing down to the water with them.

—Apostolic Tradition 21:1–5

Blood and Water

The Word of God continually calls people out of the world into a new relationship with God, with each other, and with all creation. These people are given a community, a form in which that insistent utterance of God becomes real.

Almost from the beginning, the rite of baptism, or bathing, has been that form. While it has been practiced in a marvelous diversity of ways, it is simple in its essence: after a period of instruction, new believers confess the faith of the church and are bathed in water three times, "in the name of the Father and of the Son and of the Holy Spirit." The newly baptized may be anointed with oil, clothed in new white garments, and given a candle in preparation for their immediate inclusion in the celebration of the sacred meal.

It's a ritual act with profound significations. It served as an excellent Gothic backdrop for a *Godfather* murder montage, after all. But it starts with the most ordinary things: water and words, a gathered community, and the wild diversity of people called to pass from death into life. It may be an infant in a silk gown, a father with four of his children, a retiree, or a three-year-old who attempts to maul the minister and escape the baptismal font.

In every case and by every means it is what Luther called a "public sign and a precious holy possession," establishing a new and distinct identity for God's people. Baptism is the boundary between them and the world.[1]

That new identity, that community created by baptism, has, from the beginning, been understood as a kind of family. Baptism, as a signpost of initiation and belonging, interprets both faith and family for Christians in a way that made trouble two thousand years ago and is just as radical today. Like every identity (and every family bond), it creates insiders and outsiders. But the insiders are only inside by adoption—"grace," as Christians call it. And that adoption by God challenges every boundary between insiders and outsiders.

Not everyone loves their own family, but most people—certainly most Christians—find a way to praise "the family." If baptism unites believers in something like a family, it's important to ask: What is a Christian family, anyway?

Forsaken and Taken Up

Families are at the heart of the Bible, but they don't look much like the "traditional family" we praise today. Still, it is precisely the fractured and chaotic portraits of families in the Bible that allow us to understand how powerful the identity created by baptism truly is.

In the Bible, bonds of kinship are tested, broken, and restored repeatedly. Jacob hoodwinks his twin brother, Esau, out of the birthright due the firstborn, yet they end up reconciled. Jacob's sons strand one of their number, Joseph, leaving him for dead, but he rescues them from famine in Egypt. We are meant to be shocked when Cain slays his brother, and asks God with anger and guilt if he is his brother's keeper. When the war leader Jephthah rashly promises a sacrifice that turns out to be his own daughter, we may feel something of their pain even if we can't acknowledge the father's dilemma.

Much of the Old Testament is a literal family story, from the moment God promises Abraham that his descendants—none of whom yet existed—would outnumber the stars in the darkest possible sky. It continues unbroken until the children of Abraham return from exile all numbered by their kinship.

But, as this family history unfolds, there are tantalizing interjections. Ruth, the widowed Moabite, binds herself to her Israelite mother-in-law, following her to a strange land, a strange people, and a strange God, becoming an ancestor of King David and eventually (in a way) of Jesus himself. Moses is pulled from the rushes and raised by an Egyptian princess. "If my mother and father forsake me," Psalm 27 says, "the LORD will take me up." God scatters the desire to take up and protect the forsaken among all nations and peoples. Fragile species that we are, so naked to disease and starvation and head trauma, so long in need of the care of elders, we could hardly survive without that desire.

This theme of adoption or fictive kinship, to use the anthropological term, comes dramatically to the foreground in the New Testament. Much is made of Jesus's descent from the line of David, but he is David's son only by the acknowledgment of Joseph, his guardian. He calls the people who do God's will his mother and brothers. He insists that his true followers must be willing to reject their own families and their own lives for the sake of the Gospel. He identifies the hungry, naked, foreign, and imprisoned among his followers as brothers and sisters.

Yet the more familiar images of family hardly disappear. Mary, Jesus's mother, is an awesome and abiding figure in Luke's Gospel. Paul writes tenderly of the faith passed to his disciple Timothy from his mother. A Gospel story about the man who carries Jesus's cross notes parenthetically that his sons are known to the church still.

Biological and fictive kinship intertwine throughout the Scriptures. Baptism is the quintessential expression of this duality. Yet baptism is about more than that. In the Jordan River, practiced by John the Baptist, it was a bathing of repentance. As the followers of Jesus adopt it, baptism gains meanings of death and resurrection, a washing of sins, an ark for the salvation of the faithful at the end of the age, and an initiation of many people into a single body.

Baptism places people in a new and radical relationship to each other by Christ, effected through this ancient ritual of being washed in water. And it is deeply connected to the scriptural habit of describing fellow believers as brothers and sisters.

An early Christian text, the *Didache*, roughly contemporary with the New Testament, urges the believers to mutual charity. "You must not turn away from anyone in need but share everything with your brother. . . . Remember: you are sharers in what is imperishable"—that is, the Kingdom of God—"how much more must you become sharers in what is perishable!"[2] At the same time, the *Didache* establishes baptism as a hard boundary around this community of mutual love, restricting the ritual meal of the Eucharist to those who have been baptized.

Such prohibitions seem to have been typical in early Christianity. Only the baptized in good standing were even supposed to be in the room when the holy mysteries were celebrated.

But what happened within this hard boundary of baptism was remarkable. From early on, Christian writers spoke of their religious movement as a sort of nation, a people, but unified not by blood, language, ethnicity, or class, but by their relationship with God, represented by their baptism. By this means the Gentiles would, astonishingly, be adopted into the covenant God made with Israel. Peter calls his readers "a chosen race, a royal priesthood, a holy nation." "Once you were not a people, but now you are God's people."[3] Another early source explains that Christians have no distinctive speech, customs, or dress, living in those respects like everyone around them, but live under "an extraordinary constitution of their own commonwealth."[4] This amalgamation—Jew and Greek, male and female, slave and free—was scandalous, not least to many who were part of it. This new creation of radical, familial love unbounded by blood or language was an immense and, leaving God's providence aside, unlikely achievement.

Philip, an early Jewish follower of Jesus, baptizes an Ethiopian eunuch on the road from Jerusalem. This eunuch symbolizes the social paradox of early Christianity. He is an insider as the world reckons power, a high official of his queen. But he is doubly an outsider in that less palpable kingdom where God reigns alone. First, he is a Gentile (though a God-fearing one who worships in Jerusalem). Second, he is a man sexually maimed, denied the possibility of marriage and a family of his own. Because their bodies were not whole and their status reflected pagan customs, eunuchs were ritually unclean under the Law of Moses.

But Philip finds him reading about the suffering servant depicted by Isaiah as one cut off from the future. I have always wondered about his curious position, not quite at home in any gender or class or religion, barred from the posterity of family that meant so much in his world. What was it that led him to ponder those words and, in the spiritual alchemy of the moment, to ask Philip to baptize him?

I can only imagine that Philip must have been tempted to demur, to take cautious counsel. The story could have been an embarrassment for the young Christian community. Skeptics could have mocked it as a symptom of the church's unhinged speculations about humanity and its irresponsible de-centering of identity. Maybe Philip knew he was doing something big and irreversible. That roadside stream was one of many Rubicons that Christians have faced and, sometimes haltingly, crossed. We have been meeting and crossing them so long and so consistently by now that the burden of the argument falls heavily on those who wish to remain on the near shore.

And so entering the waters—this act of baptism—marked the creation of a new identity that was held to override all other identities of blood, wealth, language, and purity. Within this new community, a kind of solidarity so radical it could only be compared to family was cultivated as the ideal relationship. In this familial solidarity, those

Entering the waters—this act of baptism—marked the creation of a new identity that was held to override all other identities of blood, wealth, language, and purity.

who are not God's people become God's people, those who are not beloved become beloved, and even a eunuch receives a family.

Back into the Water

During the centuries of Christendom, baptism became overshadowed by other sacraments as signifiers of one's status within the community. Baptism's effect was narrowed to the forgiveness of original sin. In Christian Europe, baptism was a given of life; every other identity once marginalized within its scope became more compelling. As a consequence, the community created by baptism in Christian Europe bore little resemblance to the descriptions of the church in the *Didache* or the New Testament writings.

Before the Reformation, baptism had become something like a transaction adjusting the universe's account books. It was often performed without any instruction in the faith. Interestingly, it was also the only sacrament that could be administered by laypeople, an accommodation to the fact that many children died shortly after birth and a midwife might be the only person at hand. That it was such a democratic sacrament may account in part for its low status.

Martin Luther returned baptism to a central place in Christian life. He argued that despite all the ways grace had been rationed and abused in the church of his day, baptism was still "free to all races and classes."[5] In keeping with a theological tradition maintained since the days of Augustine, he understood baptism as first and foremost the remission of sin, in the most radical terms possible. "A sinner requires, not so much to be washed, as to die," he wrote, and that dying to our sinful nature and rising to grace was a daily process vouchsafed by an unshakable promise—"not a momentary action, but something permanent."[6] He encouraged believers to make the sign of the cross each morning in remembrance of their baptism and to acknowledge their baptism with every bathing.

Beyond securing individual rebirth, Luther insisted, baptism placed Christians in a relationship of total self-giving toward each other, promising grace and imposing duties even greater than those of priestly or monastic life.

In our own time, Pope Francis has emphasized the vocation of Christian laypeople by describing the gifts conveyed by baptism as being sufficient for evangelism and Christian community. He cites the Japanese Catholics who lived for two hundred years after the expulsion of missionaries without bishops or priests, handing on the faith without ordination or the Eucharist. "When after this time other missionaries arrived again, they found all the communities in place: all baptized, catechized, all married in the church, and those who were dead, all buried in a Christian manner. There is no priest," Francis recounted in a homily. "Who did this? The baptized."[7]

Yet despite the revival of baptism, the heroic ethic of familial solidarity it once created and sustained has only been partially recovered. This is evident in movements that are trying to separate and distinguish the church from a no-longer-Christian culture and to focus their energies in teaching and service more inwardly.

In other Christian communities, especially my own more progressive Protestants, baptism is more likely to be described and practiced as a personal blessing that does not necessarily imply the definition of a community. One of my divinity school professors described splashing some water on an infant as a rather strange way to introduce him or her to the fullness of existence. It's not hard to hear the receding siren of Christendom in a view like that, an implication that baptism is simply a ritual proper to a religious tradition and not an overflowing and efficacious act of God's grace binding a person to a community of moral obligation that contains all humanity in microcosm.

Both tendencies are based in something true. Baptism really does draw a definition around the body of Christ and places us in a new relationship with each other. And it is also a freely offered gift of grace with a universal significance. When we lean too far one way, we conceive the fictive kinship of the church too narrowly, and we make its economy of grace too orderly and governed. When we lean too far the other way, we make the fictive kinship of the church more vaporous, something we merely choose for ourselves. Either way, the paradox of baptism and the new creation it signifies becomes weakened and obscured.

Outside In

This paradox of baptism—that it clearly defines a family of insiders and that it offers gratuitous love and solidarity to a world of outsiders—is especially poignant in the world today. To the extent that we as Christians grasp this holy possession, we will be forced to confront the boundaries between insiders and outsiders in the world around us.

This paradox of baptism—that it clearly defines a family of insiders and that it offers gratuitous love and solidarity to a world of outsiders—is especially poignant in the world today.

The haunting questions posed in Scripture and brought to life in baptism—"Who is my neighbor?" "Am I my brother's keeper?" "When did we see you in prison?"—have become the central questions of political debate in the democracies of the rich world. Who is inside, and who is out, when we make political decisions? Whose welfare matters?

For decades, the major ideological debates in the United States and Europe focused largely on other questions: what is the role of government in providing for citizens, and what is the role of what we call the "free market"? But in recent years, and especially since the 2008 financial collapse, our debates have been changing. Now we argue about who ought to be included in *both* government programs *and* markets. Should resident foreigners be eligible for Social Security? Should ex-felons be allowed to vote? Should migrants be allowed to hire out their labor to employers? Should people displaced by war or disaster be allowed to enter another country?

These questions are about who our communities include and who they exclude. And a resurgent and sometimes outright racist nationalism has answered them by drawing hard boundaries around ever-narrower identities. Citizens first, resident aliens second, migrants and refugees last.

But even the boundaries of national citizenship are, we increasingly find, only blurry projections of other social boundaries: race, language, religion, economic class. The move from scorning the Latino immigrant to scorning his native-born child is intuitive and quick. When there are no Muslims around to attack, it turns out that a Sikh will suffice. The American poor are no harder to stigmatize than the poor of Guatemala. Among those baptized into Christ, Scripture says, there is no longer male or female, Jew or Greek, slave or free. But even in a "Christian nation" there is very much native and immigrant, black and white, ethnic and "other," worthy and unworthy, insider and outsider. As Christians, our holy possession drowns those distinctions, but we continually face the question of whether to accept them in the policies of the nations we call home.

The staggering exodus of this decade's refugees is the most prominent way these questions of belonging and mutual obligation are posed to the old heartland of Christendom. For a time this tide of humanity and their plight was summed up in a single image of a three-year-old boy drowned on a beach in Turkey. Aylan Kurdi was his name, and he was a Kurdish Syrian attempting to escape his country's civil war with his family.

He was a stateless person. He died between nations that would not accept him, an outsider with no inside to escape to. As his miserable image rocketed around the world, it asked those of us in relatively rich, relatively safe countries whether we are his keeper, too. Christianity, this religion peopled by those having "their own commonwealth," was sometimes invoked to keep him out.

The logic of hardline nativism and nationalism finds support in the popular field of evolutionary psychology. Devotees of evolutionary psychology explain how racism and xenophobia developed as advantageous adaptations. We evolved to prefer family and extended kin groups. Ethnicities and races (which are not biological categories at all) take their shape—and their tendency toward conflict with each other—from this kinship preference. We are built by evolution to distinguish insiders from outsiders.

On the other hand, opponents of racial and ethnic nationalism respond with an ethical philosophy that insists on weighing the welfare of all humans equally. Their classic case is a child we see drowning. Surely we are obliged to act to save that child. But if that child, then why not the children we can't see? Must we not do anything and everything we can to save them, wherever and however many they may be, however unfamiliar their names or religion, whether proximity stirs our sympathy or not?

After all, from the standpoint of our shared human nature, our families, skin tones, and nationalities are as contingent as our sports allegiances. Follow the story back far enough, through migrating ancestors and conquering armies, and we're just one humanity standing at the boundary of one pleasant garden. Our distinction of insiders and outsiders is an illusion of circumstance.

This is a tough sell today. In daily life we experience our common humanity as an abstraction. Our lives are composed of circumstance. If we ever learned what sacrificial love is, we learned it from a family or something like it. If we learned pity, if was from experiencing suffering close at hand. If we learned to love sports, it was with a foam wedge of cheese on our head (for instance). Demagogues and nationalists know this very well. They know that given a choice between a particular humanity we have touched and a universal humanity we can only imagine, we'll choose the particular over and over again. The universal and impartial pretensions of our laws and philosophies don't stand a chance.

In a world torn by these competing claims, baptism is at once particular and universal. It brings outsiders in, making brothers and sisters of strangers. In a paradox, it places the center of the community at its boundary: the newly initiated are welcomed as if returning home, and the long faithful are called back again and again to that first moment of grace and adoption.

The drowned are saved and the saved are drowned. Baptism is not an in-group totem or an individual boon. It is pointing us radically outward.

In the first instance, this radicalism is about grace, not as laxity or justice at a friendly discount, but as something wholly and freely *given*. God doesn't need baptism to confer grace. But baptism summarizes all this profligacy and bestows it in the tender, intimate action of washing in water. It is perfectly contrary to the parsimony of the world, where our just deserts are continually being calculated and our structures of advantage and oppression continually rationalized and imposed on the very souls of those who live in them. The eunuch's question, "What is to prevent me from being baptized?," was not rhetorical, and Philip's answer—*Not a damn thing*—was not indulgent. The distinctions we make all drown in baptism.

In the second instance, however, baptism is radical in how we *receive* it. When we talk about the church as the "body of Christ," we're not using a metaphor for a collection of people whose sins have been graciously forgiven. It's more literal than that: Christ is present in the world in the bodies of the baptized who are being conformed to his image.

That's why it matters that we do not unite with each other through words only, but through words joined to the life-giving, universal means of our physical existence. Water was our primal home. It composes our bodies. It nourishes our lives and can snatch them away. This body, conformed to the image of Christ, has always been a rebuke to the world around it, sometimes quietly and sometimes assertively, and often enough without our knowledge.

It is no accident that Christian groups in the US and abroad are among those most steadfast in welcoming and advocating for refugees. It's true that this body can become a focus of ugly, exclusive nationalist politics. But as far as it retains that image, that body—and it always somehow retains it, in unshakable words and inescapable grace—it repeats the generosity of Christ without any regard for what we or anyone else deserves.

When Jesus feeds the multitudes with loaves and fish, he doesn't scrutinize them for hidden assets, bad motives, or documents out of order; he doesn't condemn a Samaritan woman living in an irregular domestic arrangement; and when he's asked "Who is my neighbor?," he tells a story about a man who crosses ethnic and religious boundaries to help a stranger left for dead. To be conformed to the image of Christ in the world is not to deny love of place and family and community. To be conformed to the image of Christ is to imaginatively apply that love to people who have no such bonds of circumstance with us. Baptism is given not to an ideal humanity, but to imperfect humans, and it charges and empowers them to love each other as their own imperfect flesh.

Hence the final, irresolvable paradox of baptism: it defines a community whose boundary is its practice of being unbounded. It defines a family whose limit is its practice of transcending limits. It creates what Augustine called "a society of aliens."[8]

In my experience, we are often very bad at embracing this paradox. Racism and economic inequality continue to raise some very high walls within and between our churches. But the fulfillment is already latent in Christian communities, often in small or even embarrassing ways. Progressives have been known to mock conservative, "traditional" churches of an evangelical persuasion for the prevalence of divorced or single-parent households among their adherents. But this is a glorious thing, even if the churches themselves don't witness to its glory very reliably. It attests to the power of grace in forming and sustaining those communities. Conservatives likewise have been known to mock mainline churches for their familial respectability (especially when this respectability is defined to include same-sex families), as if that stability and commitment weren't the root and school of love for others. Christians are, to a degree that would probably shock their cultured despisers, already resisting the modern urge to fragment humanity into competing kin groups, or to lose humanity to abstraction. We just don't always know it.

Orphan Species and Foundling People

We baptized my first son in a gown made from the silk of my long-departed grandfather's parachute—not one of the two that saved his life during the Second World War, but the one Uncle Sam gave him as a parting gift at the end of it. When, late in life, he finally unburdened himself about the war, he couldn't seem to imagine forgiveness for the bombs he'd dropped on the women conscripted to defend an oil depot in Romania, or the people he'd killed up close when he was an escaped prisoner of war.

I never talked about baptism with him. I don't think he was ever taught to see it in the pious foster mother, the only woman he ever called by that name, who took him in when she could have excluded him as a threat or a burden. I don't think he connected the symbolic plunge he took as an infant to the dying and rising he sought up to the end of his life. He and the Lord were not on speaking terms after the war, but the Lord did indeed take him up when he was forsaken, and if the improbability of his survival is any evidence, the Lord never quite left him. His presence, in that parachute, made Soren's baptism bittersweet and ironic. As all baptisms are: God's grace poured out like tears for a humanity that would prefer to get by without it.

We became foster parents not long after. One day, an infant girl showed up at our house, as foster children do today, with some clothes in a plastic bag and a state insurance card (renewed monthly, to prevent anyone getting more health care than they are entitled to). My wife and I busied ourselves with making medical appointments, caring for a child whose only vocalization was a bark-stripping shriek, and enduring the gnomish humiliations in store for clients of the welfare state. But our son set to work on having a sister. He did this—sudden-onset sibling rivalry not withstanding—with the virtuosity of feeling possible only for children, saints, and fools.

Adults who commit to nurturing an unrelated child through sleepless nights and unrelenting screams have to fake it till they make it. It was, truly, a daily dying to self and rising to God for my wife and me. We had to hold on to our abstract sense of duty through a drought of the parental feelings we associated with our biological child. Children, on the other hand, make it long before they learn that faking it is possible. I would be at wit's end trying to calm a wheezing eighteen-month-old who would have no part of waiting for the doctor, but Soren would hold her tight and say, "I love you, Sophia, I love you," and immediately she would fall silent.

But make it we did. Eventually, the space marked out by our commitment was filled with a love no less fierce than what we knew with Soren. The biblical Hebrew word we translate as "steadfast love" is more a matter of steadfastness than love, as we tend to think of it. The gift of love is added to perseverance. The church helped too, with bags of clothes and pans of lasagna and babysitting and doting of every kind on our fast-bound children.

Soren knew as early as he could that Sophia was his foster sister, that she had other parents who saw her every week. When she was reunited with her mother, after more than two years, he took it even harder than we did. "I used to have a sister—now I don't have a sister," he'd say. Or worse, "We tried to pray for Sophia, but it didn't work." But this too resolved, with the hardness of a four-year-old stung by the world. "She's my sister," he would insist fiercely when anyone misunderstood or qualified their relationship, which, of course, she was and is and always will be. Her coming and her going, and the bond that endured, was our education in the meaning of our baptism.

All love, all family, all circumstance is just as beautiful, tragic, and arbitrary. Adoption—an outsider becoming an insider—is in everyone's lineage somewhere if you follow it back far enough. Someone's parents never came home. Someone was left on a doorstep or taken home from an orphan train. Someone was taken up and washed and clothed by strange hands, an orphan whose only family was a new creation.

Adoption—an outsider becoming an insider—is in everyone's lineage somewhere if you follow it back far enough.

What we learn from the fictive family of baptism is that our own blood ties, the fruit of our own bodies, are just as much a random and gratuitous gift as a child who turns up on the doorstep. And the child on the doorstep is bound to us as tightly and necessarily as the child we bear. We are an orphan species, cast upon the spinning world at random. But as a new creation, we are a foundling people.

This new creation, this family of foundlings, is gathered by the Word and identified and incorporated by baptism. This family is washed together, fed together, reconciled together, and joined in prayer and song together. In grasping and acting on these shared practices, this family doesn't become just one more identity in a world riven by class and ethnicity. It enacts a way of being that resists and undermines every power of division and hostility around it.

Chapter 3

MEAL

A World in Miniature

> Presider: *Lord, I am not worthy that you should come under my roof.*
> People: *But only say the word, and my soul shall be healed.*
>
> —Eucharistic liturgy

Fruit and Work

Martha was an old woman dying in a room in Bridgeport who wanted communion. As I fed her this last wafer, I noticed she bore an uncanny resemblance to my late grandmother. Then, mouth slowly rotating around the body of Christ, she simply failed to swallow it. My grandmother was going to asphyxiate on Jesus, and it would be my fault. I tried to rescue her from Him, and Him from her, pouring dread into the poor woman's late moment of devotion. Eventually a desultory home health aide and a glass of water helped mollify both me and the sacrament, and she swallowed it safely.

Helen never met me before her dementia took over and couldn't remember me between visits, but her face always lit up when I offered her the sacrament, and after she received it, she always fixed me with a stare and told me, gravely and lucidly, "I love you."

Albert slipped out of mid-week Mass at the Episcopal cathedral with dispatch so he could hit up departing fellow-communicants for money. After saying no a few times, I started using my food stamps to buy us both lunch at the nearby Whole Foods. He kept his belongings at the Pacific Garden Mission, but as a younger man he made a lot of money drywalling before his girlfriend shot him three times in the back with a .38 handgun. "Now I've got nothing," he told me, but he was happy.

Betty was always perfectly dressed and coifed at church. She was also a compulsive winker. Even the Sunday after her husband died, following a swift and terrible illness, she was impeccable, smiling and winking. But when she came forward for communion and heard "the Body of Christ, given for you," her face relaxed into grief and tears.

A meal is not simply food, any more than a word is simply sound. What that food is, how and where it reaches us, who we do and don't share it with, what relationships it establishes, strengthens, or breaks in the eating—all of these make a meal. To turn the stuff of mere survival into community, culture, even art is a quintessentially human thing. In one liturgical prayer we offer the bread for the holy Christian meal to God as "fruit of the earth and work of human hands," and so it is. A mutation in the DNA of a wild grass makes it into wheat, which long domestication and the genius of grinding, adding water, and applying fire turn into bread. It's something like a miracle.

In their Gospels, Mark and Matthew put two big meals side by side. The first is a feast thrown by King Herod for his birthday. He plays host to courtiers and officials, and his stepdaughter dances so pleasingly for him and his guests that he stirs himself to make her a rash promise: Ask for anything, and it's yours. So she asks for the head of John the Baptist (absent from the great event because he was imprisoned for his imprudent preaching against the king's marriage) served up on a platter. Honor—the social bond reinforced by the great public display of a banquet—requires a fearful Herod to follow through.

In the next passage Jesus encounters a vast crowd of the sort of people not typically invited to royal banquets. They were, in fact, crashing what was to be a private and restful meal with his disciples. He teaches the crowd, who appeared as sheep without a shepherd, and then resists the commonsensical recommendation by his disciples that they be sent away to buy food for themselves. Instead, Jesus feeds the people himself, five thousand men and an unrecorded number of women and children, with five loaves and two fish.

The first meal is lavish, the second almost pitiably simple. The first is strictly invitation-only—John the Baptist, prominent though he was, could only get in on a platter—while the second is open to all. Herod exercises tyrannical power while Jesus acts as a shepherd. One dissolves in a shocking parody of a feast; the other ends with shocking abundance. One turns on a promise that leads to death; the other foreshadows a promise that leads to life. Each meal is a world in miniature.

So it goes throughout the Gospels. At the table, religion is argued, guests are repelled or included, conflicts are revealed or mended. The company is either godly or sinful. The whole Bible is framed by meals, from guilty fruit shared secretly in Genesis to the wedding feast of the Lamb in Revelation. In between, meals are the site of miracles and the image of prophetic anticipations. God will host all the nations on the holy mountain and feast them with old wine and fat meat.

The whole Bible is framed by meals, from guilty fruit shared secretly in Genesis to the wedding feast of the Lamb in Revelation.

In between the stories and the hopes, Jesus shares a meal with his friends on the night before his arrest. The accounts do not agree in every detail, but we see Jesus giving thanks, sharing the bread, saying, "This is my body," and the cup of wine, saying, "This is my blood," and leaving a command to "do this in remembrance of me." Like the Passover depicted in Exodus, this meal (which may or may not have taken place on the Passover) made the jump from being a story *about* the world to being an action that *shaped* the world. And it has for Christians and through Christians ever since.

Meeting and Eating

Through words God calls people, and through water God gives them a new family and a new identity. Through the third holy possession, the sacred meal Christians share, we move from identity to actions—from who we are to what we do.

From the beginning, considerable diversity marked what we do when we share this bread and wine.[1] In fact, so much diversity existed that if there is a convincing account of how the meal, variously known as Eucharist, Mass, Holy Communion, Lord's Supper, and more, developed into the forms recorded in histories and worship books, I haven't read it. But it seems to have been, at first, part of an actual meal celebrated by Christians gathered in homes. In these meal gatherings, Christ was made present in bread and wine and in the church—male and female, Jew and Greek, slave and free, rich and poor—united in peace, fellowship, and expectation.

Many aspects of early Christian practice faded away or spun off into separate rituals. But at the heart of this action were a community, bread and wine, and the ineffable presence of Jesus of Nazareth. Those proved remarkably resilient. Of course, you can't practice something for two thousand years without some dramatic changes and conflicts. Those conflicts, caused by politics, philosophy, and scriptural interpretation, gathered with that church around the meal from the earliest days.

The migration of Christianity into new regions and cultures saw this ritual lose, gain, or shift meanings. The meal setting slipped away. It took on characteristics of Roman sacrificial offerings. The shared table of a Mediterranean home was replaced by a ritual table in a basilica, which itself grew higher and farther from the people. Ritual distance reflected (and perhaps begat) theological distance. Once Christians became rather too common in the earth, the conjoined holiness of the people, the event, and the bread and wine started to fray. The holiness of the whole meal held fast in the things, the consecrated elements. The bread and wine became the unique and particular location of divine presence and power.

Not until we'd been at it for the better part of a millennium did Christians start to argue in earnest over what the bread and wine really *were* in the Eucharist. In Jesus's words "This is my body," what does the "is" actually do? How do we account for both Christ's promise to be present in a bodily way and the evident breadiness of the bread? The answer the Western church settled upon in the thirteenth century was the doctrine of transubstantiation, by which the form or "accidents" of the bread remain, while the essence or "substance" of bread turns into Christ's human body at the words of the priest. The shadow side of this intensity of Christ's presence in the things was that, in the popular imagination, the bread of the Eucharist became a sort of charmed object.

Ingenious though the doctrine of transubstantiation was and is, dissents were always present. The Reformation unleashed a multitude of alternative interpretations, some old, some new. When Martin Luther began making proposals for church reform, he didn't attack transubstantiation, arguing more narrowly that the philosophy that underwrote the doctrine shouldn't be mandatory for Christian faith. His main concerns were with the withholding of the cup from the people, and some practices that had grown up around the sacrament that seemed unnecessary or irreverent.

Others, however, went farther—sometimes much farther. The ghosts of those arguments linger around our altars and communion tables still. Yet it's in the nature of a religious ritual to preserve itself despite the best efforts of those who practice it. Some Protestants who hold to a purely symbolic view of the bread and wine nonetheless hand it down from a high and distant Gothic altar. A greeting (formerly a kiss) of peace among the worshipers lingers in many places, however high and hierarchical the liturgy, as a reminder that we were once sharing a meal in an intimate space among friends. However rarified the arguments become, and however far the practices wander from anything recognizable to the people keeping the Passover in that Jerusalem room, they tend to come back to the same questions that can, and maybe should, be asked of any meal: What do we eat? Who are we eating with?

Real Presence

Charismatic Swiss priest Ulrich Zwingli was an early proponent of the view that Christ was not present in the bread and wine because his body was in heaven and, in any case, physical flesh can't do any good for a person's spiritual condition.

Against Zwingli, Luther defended the real presence of Christ's body and blood in the meal, with a vigor that approaches comedy and at a length that taxes even the zealous student. Luther's response comes down to two main contentions, one about God and one about human beings. First, the human body of Jesus can't be separated from his divine nature, because if it were, the result would be a "poor sort of Christ" available only in one place, and a "mere isolated God" separated from humanity—and a Christ so circumscribed would himself need a savior![2] Second, human faith needs to be strong and, borrowing a word from other theologians, *absurd* enough to trust God's works as God promises them, not as we are able to perceive or understand them.

The upshot is that Christ, as human and as God, is literally omnipresent in creation. The body of Christ is everywhere by virtue of its union with his divinity, and it becomes explicit and available to us through his command and promise to eat his flesh and drink his blood in the Eucharist. This is, as Luther himself makes clear, a pretty mind-bending idea. Not that everything *is* the body of Christ—that would be pantheism. Rather, he argues that all things are "permeable and present to him."[3]

> If Christ sat at one place in the center of the universe, like the bubble or spark in a crystal, and if a certain point in the universe were indicated to me, as the bread and wine are set forth to me by the Word, should I not be able to say, "See, there is

> the body of Christ actually in the bread," just as I say, when a certain side of the crystal is placed before my eyes, "See, there is the spark in the very front of the crystal"?[4]

This notion is, to use the technical theological term, trippy. That the solid-seeming world is permeable to Christ's body like a sponge to water, or that all creatures are transparent to Christ's body like a gem to its flaw, and that in either case it's not our perceptions or modes of understanding that define the limits of our faith but the reliability of God's promise. Looking back through the centuries at Luther's argument, we encounter the meal not as a shipwrecked traveler from an age of magic and miracles, but as a re-imagining of the relationship between the world and God.

We encounter the meal not as a shipwrecked traveler from an age of magic and miracles, but as a re-imagining of the relationship between the world and God.

I've never understood the conviction that Christ's body is really *absent* from the meal. There are so many places in the world and moments in life and gatherings of humanity where Christ is impossible for human reason to perceive; I can't see the purpose in highlighting his own memorial celebration in order to say, "Wherever Christ really is, it isn't in these things." This isn't because I am an athlete in faith, but rather the opposite. When I was a new Christian, I sought out the bread and wine almost compulsively, darting into weekday churches at morning, noon, or nightfall to tide me over between Sundays and stepping out into a world made bright with tears and the hot flush of blood in my face.

Sara Miles poignantly recalls the dissonance between "what I heard someone else say was happening—the piece of bread was the 'body' of 'Christ,' a patently untrue or at best metaphorical statement; and what I knew was happening—God, named 'Christ' or 'Jesus,' was real, and in my mouth." And she's hardly alone. The immediacy of the experience of eating and drinking can clash so loudly with the operations of the mind that one might almost speculate that the dissonance is intended.

The bread is permeable to a Galilean God-man, and it becomes part of us. In the act, we see that we are permeable to the same Jesus. Receiving the sacrament and experiencing this dissonance, Miles writes, "utterly short-circuited my ability to do anything but cry."[5] Weeping is not the only suitable response, but it's a perfectly rational one.

Philosopher Charles Taylor, who literally wrote the book on our "secular age," describes modern European/North American people as "buffered selves," strongly individuated and distinct from each other and the world around us. This is by contrast to the "porous selves" of traditional or religious societies, who understand themselves as susceptible to a variety of friendly or hostile outside forces. This is only true up to a point; to believe oneself "buffered" from the world is not a universal experience among modern "secular" people. But it's fair to say that it's an aspiration. We may not *be* immune to attacks of trauma or mass hysteria or collective manipulation—modern equivalents to the demonic attacks suffered by people before secularity came along—but some of us may *feel* immune, and most of the rest of us seem to wish to be.

The meal threatens this aspiration. To bodily receive not just something divine, but something human—an itinerant crucified Jewish preacher of the heavenly kingdom on earth who is also God—is a destabilizing experience. Just as the Word confronts us with our ideological limitations and baptism challenges the givenness of our loyalties, the meal breaks down barriers within and without that we may prefer not to notice, much less transcend. Permeable bodies in a hard-edged world find trouble.

The intimate union of Christ's humanity and divinity, and the intimate union of the communicant with Christ, take the permeability of the believer into new territory. Christ is really present in the moment, but so are other bodies. The meal is what we eat, and also who we eat with.

This experience of fellowship can have an erotic element that underscores the radical and potentially dangerous meaning of "communion." It was more than mere misunderstanding that made early critics of Christian worship suspect that sexual immorality was central to this new religion. Sex, like the sharing of food, is thronged with anxieties about social and biological complications. It is no accident that Christian sex education so frequently relies on the image of the same piece of gum being chewed by many people. (I haven't looked into it empirically, but I'd guess that churches that tell their young people that having sex with more than one partner is like passing chewing gum from mouth to mouth don't have especially intimate communion practices, either.) Cultivating disgust at the permeable borders between people is a powerful way to keep their affections and loyalties locked within. The medieval mystics and ascetics kissed the wounds of lepers, had erotic visions of union with Christ at the altar, drank his blood from a shared cup. Had we all imitated them, either the world would have collapsed or utopia would have emerged. One reason modern culture appears to be so saturated with sexuality is that sex offers a rare escape from our profound fear of each other.

That fear is fully on display in contemporary communion practices. Christians in the US, like US citizens in general, are obsessed with health and hygiene. Pasteurized grape juice was invented in the US and came to displace wine in many Protestant celebrations of communion. And I can't say for sure, but I'd bet a significant sum that we invented those tiny individual cups, too—pre-filled for sanitary personal consumption and disposable by the thousand where washing and reusing prove too burdensome. It's a strange fate for things that were meant to be shared and that were intended to become, or at least to signify, a human body.

I've received communion in most ways it can be received, from the sludgier common chalices to the antiseptically sealed single servings of juice and wafer. I'm most accustomed to the difference-splitting practice we call intinction, which involves dipping the bread into the chalice. People seem to find this comforting compared to drinking from a common cup, but that's probably because they don't see as many fingernails as I do. Cracked, dirty, untended fingernails plunging eagerly into the blood of Christ. It must be a trick of perception, but I'm convinced that the dirtier the fingernail, the further in it goes.

Fear of biological contagion is hard to distinguish from fear of social contagion. When AIDS, which is not communicated by saliva, reached epidemic levels, some churches responded with panic and anger. The act of eating and drinking together doesn't look especially intimate until it implies the possibility of sharing a disease or a social status. Taking the risk, however modest, of sharing pathogens is a form of social solidarity, an acceptance of each other that can touch very deep insecurities.

That is the other, essential real presence in the meal: unchosen others, with their problems, their histories, their potentially contagious microbiomes. When we eat together, we are wreathed and entangled in all of it. We do everything we can to separate ourselves, if we've been given the economic and political power to do so. Our housing policy and financial system work to segregate our neighborhoods; our infrastructure and our gated communities route us in or keep us out; our rules for health and hygiene and panhandling demand visible conformity.

The church has too often passively accepted or actively promoted all this social segregation. Yet humanity creeps in through the seams, and once there, around that table, resistance is wounded. This holy possession brings together people who would otherwise never meet, much less share something so intimate as a meal. As the historical theologian Thomas O'Loughlin put it: "The breaching of the boundaries of Graeco-Roman society at this Christian meal is one of the miracles of the early Church."[6] It's a miracle of the church today, too. The breaching of boundaries between people cannot help but send a minor tremor through the whole social order.

Being What We Eat

Our desire to find or make meaning in what we eat—that charmingly human, perhaps fundamentally religious impulse—hasn't gone away. It's just shifted to other things. Our food has always been a locus for luxury and moral delicacy, but perhaps never more than in our seemingly secular age. Our phones are the products of heinous destruction, but our chocolate can be, for the right price, sustainably produced, fairly traded, and ritually authenticated. Even as a delusion this isn't all bad—the alternative is chocolate (or coffee, or beef, or anything) churned forth by the same exorbitant processes that give us in the rich world a false sense of abundance. If humans are, as philosopher Ludwig Feuerbach wrote, what they eat, it is poignant that we will bear some cost to eat goodness, or at least blamelessness, real or fraudulent. Perhaps, buffered as we are, we are still hungry for God.

At the same time, displacing our anxieties and scruples about all of moral life into our food can easily create a false purity, located solely in what we eat rather than who eats with us, and what happens around us as we do. Every meal is a picture of the world in which it takes place, and an obsession with the *what* creates a deceptive picture. Good consumption is still, in the end, consumption, available only to those who can afford it. Imagine Herod consoling himself, as the hideous platter is taken away, that at least all the produce was locally sourced.

The power of the sacrament reaches us from the opposite direction. The *what* is perfectly undistinguished—plain bread, a plain body. It takes place in and with the bloody and broken and spittle-flecked world, apart from any illusion that bread is earned without the sweat of Adam's face, or that those sharing it have left their needs, wounds, or peculiar sins at the door of the church. It is the sheer marvel of humans eating together, gathered in a mingling of social statuses and bacteria, an unexampled proximity of kneeling and breath and tears. It defies a world whose tables are divided by mutual fear and suspicion. And since people will continue to be hungry and lonely and imprisoned (in themselves if nowhere else), to serve and be served, to eat and be eaten, God will continue to feed them.

Chapter 4

CONFESSION AND FORGIVENESS

Far from the Tree

> PEOPLE: *I confess to God Almighty, before the whole company of heaven, and to you, my brothers and sisters, that I have sinned in thought, word, and deed by my fault, by my own fault, by my own most grievous fault; wherefore I pray God Almighty to have mercy on me, forgive me all my sins, and bring me to everlasting life. Amen.*
>
> OFFICIANT: *The almighty and merciful Lord grant you pardon, forgiveness, and remission of all your sins. Amen.*
>
> —COMPLINE

Sin, Table for One

Smoking is not enumerated by most Christians as an actual sin. But smoking is what taught me what sin is. It's one of the worst things you can do to yourself; I've known that since I started following my parents around badgering them to quit. It empties your wallet, squeezes your lungs, sparks lethal mutations in your cells, and wards decent company away. I miss it almost every day.

For me, cigarettes are terminals in a vast, dense network of remembered experience. A whiff outside of a downtown office building can pick me up and drop me, momentarily, who knows where: in the desert rolling loose-leaf, on the quad palpitating from a class, or drinking instant coffee on a balcony in Taiwan. Many of those places and moments would otherwise be lost because they were otherwise vacant. They were idle moments before the descent of smartphones and omnipresent media. A break came in work, or between sets, or before the day ended or began. Not long ago, a break in a class or meeting meant a chance to stand up, leave the building, light a little fire (alone or in a circle), and inhale deeply. We scarcely ever take deep breaths.

Now these moments are spent inhaling through screens. Rather than an invitation to a little self-destructive idleness, a break is an opportunity to scroll through notifications, share and like, scan for urgent or diverting communications. They're unremembered because they happen, truly, nowhere. Where were you when you first saw the "Winter is Coming" meme from *Game of Thrones*? The class or task proves to have been the break, the stepping out of the digital stream in which we swim, the unharnessing from the algorithms that sit astride our lives.

There is all of that. And then there's the bit where I'm still, in a sense, addicted. Nicotine fiddles with your brain chemistry in a way that is apparently very long-lasting, maybe permanent. Maybe a genetic variation predisposes people to become addicted to nicotine, and if one does, a glance at my family history strongly suggests I have it. Even once the cravings are gone, the capacity for pleasure doesn't go away. It's there, already primed to answer the bell and both flood me with dopamine and snap me back to some sunny day outside the Sacramento bus station when anything was, in principle, possible.

That an action as debilitating and deadly as smoking can prey on us like this, weaving together the warp of our brain chemistry and the woof of our memory, creativity, and sociability, says something remarkable about human beings. We cooperate with our own destruction, not by demonic possession or malfunctioning software but with the finest tunings of our minds. Our best and our worst, our weakness and our strength always seem to travel together, even to feed off each other in a bloody, gasping symbiosis. The same habitual action can make us both Marcel Proust recollecting his childhood and a lab rat frantically punching the reward bar.

I never smoked a cigarette I didn't want to smoke, but I didn't want, or even choose, the *compulsion* to smoke. This is the dynamic Augustine had in mind when he tried to explain how the human will, after the Fall of Adam and Eve, is bound by sin: "Man's wretchedness is nothing but his own disobedience to himself, so that because he would not do what he could, he now wills to do what he cannot."[1] It's certainly possible to resolve to quit; in theology this is called "repentance." And it's possible, with time and effort, to alter one's habits; this is what we call "regeneration" or "amendment of life." But it isn't within anyone's power to will a compulsion away or to keep those neurons from standing ready, at a moment's notice, to bathe you in the sweet oblivion of relapse. So it is, the sages have taught us over the centuries, with all of life's moral choices: an evil may be chosen in full knowledge, at the noble urging of desire, sentiment, even virtue, and yet not chosen freely, and less freely the more it is chosen.

As it goes with each of us, so much the more with great systems. Tobacco changed the world. Europe's craving for it (and sugar cane, another delight that big swathes of humanity got by without for a long time) helped create the Atlantic slave trade, the brutally rational and efficient system of plantation slavery that dominated large parts of the Americas, and the American financial system and modern capitalism.

So it happened that a specific desire that was unknown in much of the world until quite recently could become so urgent that, with enough money and technology, people would force mass migration and unpaid labor to fulfill it. Then they would invent mass production of pre-rolled cigarettes, making smoking cheap and convenient enough to transform a modest vice into a global public health catastrophe, with one hundred fifty million disability-adjusted life-years lost to tobacco in the year 2015.[2]

One of the memorable public moments of my youth was the sight of executives from all the American tobacco companies saying, under oath, that their product wasn't addictive. It's strange to watch people saying something that both they and every single person listening knows is false. But what should they have done? The honorable thing would have been to demolish their own industry from within. But if you're employed by that industry, pointing out that tobacco companies are piloting a pirate ship made of human skulls will just get you thrown overboard. The ship of desire will roll on, regardless of the perfidy or heroism of one executive.

It's hard to tell a lie in full knowledge that you won't actually deceive anyone, even yourself. Given the chance, most of us take our place somewhere, great or small, in the operation of the world's evils. A lot of us want to convince ourselves that it's a virtue. My little IRA is funding and profiting from God-knows-what all around the world. I take a small bit of bourgeois satisfaction in my automatic monthly contributions all the same, strive toward them, squirrel away more when it comes. If we opt out, or get thrown out through some act of courage, we can all be replaced. That's what systems are for.

Yet at the apex of these systems of destruction and exploitation we see, with striking frequency, such fineness of character and moral sentiment. From Thomas Jefferson to the Greenwich Humane Society, there is a kind of moral grandeur that makes good on the outrageous advantages such a stricken world provides. To compensate for them. Or to hide them, if from no one but ourselves. We are good people. At any rate, we are not bad people.

Origin Stories

At the heart of all the "holy possessions" of the church we've explored sit sin and forgiveness. The Word can be seen as revealing sin and offering the promise of forgiveness. Baptism makes this promise effective by water and the faith of the believer. And the meal comes as a continuing pledge of this forgiveness, received by faith and strengthening faith. But it's the fourth possession, the "office of the keys" or confession and absolution, that focuses our attention specifically and insistently on sin. This holy possession demonstrates what it means to name, confess, and reprove sin, to have it forgiven, and in both the confession and the forgiveness, for Christians to be named as "a holy people."[3]

From a certain point of view, sin is the characteristic problem of humankind. Other than the angels, nothing else in Creation is capable of it, or so we say. The problem is not merely that we act and suffer to our own harm and each other's—everything does that, even galaxies (we're set to collide with the Andromeda galaxy in about 4.5 billion years, so sell your real estate before then). It's that we create, ruminate on, amplify that harm, to such an extent that we experience it as a Problem, not merely a fact of everyday life but an exile, an estrangement, a loss so deep we can't remember when it happened. Sin isn't an action or even a habit of mind, but a condition; it's living on the other side. The path back to the Garden of Eden is blocked to us with a flaming sword.

Sin isn't an action or even a habit of mind, but a condition; it's living on the other side. The path back to the Garden of Eden is blocked to us with a flaming sword.

Myths of this primal, permanent exile are not uniquely Christian. Both ancient and modern schools of thought have tried to explain them. To modern-day social Darwinists, we're lab rats whose brains overshot the mark in devising ways to get food and sex, burdening us with the capacity for guilt and remorse. Or else, perhaps the guilt and remorse are just more refined tools for getting food and sex, which totally contradicts the first explanation but is similarly efficient. For Plato, it starts with a fall from the realm of true being; for Marx, with the development of property relations; for Freud, with the primal trauma. As far as they go, they are all haunting ways to re-describe a mystery and call it an explanation.

Nor is the Christian "explanation" in the third chapter of Genesis terribly convincing, either. There was a tree, and a serpent persuades the first woman and first man to eat a piece of the fruit of that tree to gain knowledge of Good and Evil, to open their eyes and become like God. So our sojourn in Eden ends with the pronouncement that we will quarrel with snakes and each other, that we will have to work for our bread and suffer in childbirth and return to dust at the last. It's what scholars call an etiology, a legendary origin story for facts we observe in the world.

Making it properly "theological" has always been a bit of a chore. What precisely was the sin of the first couple? Lust for the fruit? Disobedience of the divine command? Pride and envy? Were we lab rats who punched the bar too hard, or who broke the rules of the experiment, or who tried to take over the lab itself? Does this event continue in human life through procreation, or only by our imitating it—by genes or by "memes"? Did the fateful fruit, once digested, alter our chemistry? Did it change the fabric of Creation, or did it just change humanity? And anyway, doesn't it suggest some prior inclination to sin latent in the man and the woman, just waiting to be triggered by the snake's smooth words, like brain cells waiting for that postlapsarian wash of nicotine?

I've read a few books on sin. I've supplemented my reading with extensive field research. And I'll admit I don't have a way to make this story work as an actual explanation for the existence of what we call sin. But within the mythic dimensions of the story there is an eloquent and very human drama. The serpent approaches the woman with a question: "Did God say, 'You shall not eat of any tree in the garden'?" When she confirms the prohibition of the one tree, on pain of death, the serpent attempts a misdirection. "You will not die," it tells her, "for God knows that when you eat of it your eyes will be opened, and you will be like God, knowing good and evil." There must have been some mistake. God didn't mean to stand in the way of knowledge. So the woman sees that, in addition to being attractive and bearing delicious fruit, "the tree was to be desired to make one wise," and she and the man eat. And in their first experience of moral knowledge, the man and the woman become ashamed of their bodies and clothe themselves. The new day dawns not with moral progress, nor even with the unfettered joy of willful rebellion, but with self-estrangement.

To make matters worse, when God appears, they hide, being estranged from him as well as from themselves. And they rationalize. The man blames the woman. The woman blames the snake. Augustine called it "the pride shown in the search for an excuse, even when the sins are clear as daylight."[4] Thus human history is off and running with the pointless whinge of those who have been caught out.

So if this fable isn't exactly an explanation for sin, it is at least a remarkably sophisticated picture of how it works. It says less about what we do than about why we do it—to gain knowledge and become wise—and especially what stories we tell about it—"She made me!" And it says a lot about the world we made, or found, so shot-through with alienation. We're alienated from our bodies, which we cover; from each other, starting even in our families; from the earth, from which we must wrestle our survival, by increasingly severe means; and from God, from whom we hide. Luther, in a somewhat Romantic frame of mind, described the Tree as the center of the first church, where an innocent humanity would have gathered on the Sabbath to praise God's goodness in creation:

> If they had not fallen into sin, Adam would have transmitted this single command later on to all his descendants. From it would have come the best theologians, the most learned law-

> yers, and the most expert physicians. Today there is an infinite number of books for instruction of theologians, lawyers, and physicians; but whatever we learn with the help of books hardly deserves to be called dregs in comparison with that wisdom which Adam drew from this single Word. So corrupt has everything become through original sin.[5]

It's a sign of how seriously Luther, following Augustine, took sin that he identified the development of *good things* in human life as its fruit. Elaboration replaces simplicity, striving replaces receiving, learning replaces knowledge. The perversity in the promise that the fruit would make us like God is that we would demand more than life gave us, and yet, paradoxically, we would accept less.

Christians, starting with Paul the Apostle, crafted rhetorical parallels for this story with the life and death of Jesus, where the forbidden Tree of Knowledge is overcome by the atoning Tree of the Cross, and the sinful Adam is redeemed by the sinless New Adam.

But the problem, being solved in principle and in the big story, still persists in the midst of things. People are still intransigent. I've had congregants, for example, tell me they're going to do things they will never do, and want some credit or at least assurance for the sake of those never-to-be-done things. Like a boat tethered to a dock, I batter repeatedly against my own limits in loving them, answering my call to serve them, and facing my own sins. I'm convinced that they and I will be the exception to the general rule of human alienation and excuse. I'm also convinced that it will not be my fault if we aren't.

There must be some promise for us in our daily enactment of that business with the tree. That's where the office of the keys comes in. What does it mean to forgive a real, live sinner embedded in a whole fabric of personal and social and global disasters? And how does that act foreshadow and bring about an alternative reality for the world?

Grasping Forgiveness

The office of the keys has been on an adventure almost as long and winding as the meal. It has enduring elements. It has always required a spoken confession by the penitent, who laments her sin and seeks comfort and restoration. This is answered in a spoken absolution from God through a minister.[6] We see these, though not necessarily side by side, in the Gospels.

Two other elements are more variable but also enduring. One is the penance or satisfaction. Early on, penitents adopted formal signs such as ashes, sackcloth, and postures of supplication. Later, penance was calibrated to the specific offense—fasting for gluttons, abstinence for the lecherous—or aimed toward spiritual direction and teaching, in which some change in the mind-set and habits of the penitent was sought alongside the confession of sin and the restoration to grace.[7]

The second element is some gesture or ritual action that seals the absolution. Laying hands on the penitent as a sign of pardon was one. Others included signing with the cross and placing the end of the priest's stole on the penitent.

Custom and culture shrank and shifted this holy possession, as they did the great immersion in running water and the solemn, festive Christian meal. The practice of the keys required trade-offs and compromises. The severity of penitence had to be balanced with accessibility for everyday sinners and everyday sins. The role of the community contended with the desire of individuals for privacy. The practice could focus on acts or on inclinations. It could focus on routine and private or grave and public sins. By the time Luther came along, confession to a priest was mandatory at least once a year, and it had to be "general"—that is, comprehensive—to the best of the sinner's ability.

This was a problem for Luther. He thought that it was impossible to enumerate all your sins, or even to know you'd made your best effort to do so. The spiritual economy of sin and forgiveness was intricate. Was a sinner seeking forgiveness out of fear of punishment, or out of love for God? Did the forgiveness of eternal guilt leave a penalty that needed to be paid in purgatory, and could that penalty itself be remitted in other ways? Luther simplified this economy radically. He focused on two things: the sinner's repentance, provoked by God's righteous judgment, and the sinner's trust, provoked by God's gracious promise.

As a result, Lutheran theology and practice gained an existential starkness at the same time it lost valuable insights. Sin, deep and vexing condition that it is, prompted splendid innovation in cures. Some were pure quackery, but some involved discoveries of Nobel-level medicine. Ignatius of Loyola, a rough contemporary of Luther, founder of the Jesuit order and a total boss, developed a method for identifying and tracking sins as they happened and reducing them through deliberate attention. There's an app for this now.

Yet none of these treatments, Luther's included, was a cure any more than the theologies of sin were an explanation. "Oh, we shall allow them even sin," Dostoyevsky's Grand Inquisitor tells Christ, and who can deny the truth of it?[8] Adultery in the eyes, murder in the heart, a stray hand in the till enacted and absolved unto the end of the age. The gaping human self-estrangement from all that exists had to be parceled, weighed, and packaged on the scale of a solution. Meanwhile, the tobacco plantations needed to yield their increase and the portfolios their returns. The real work of the world happened as it always did—by bombs and swords and surveillance and wealth and ideas deployed and discarded as the world needed them.

Even where we've rejected the mysterious cosmic accounting of sin and forgiveness, sin travels under many names and has many solutions. For our compulsions we have treatments. For our excesses we undertake quantified cleanses and purgations. Our social privilege can be "checked" by ourselves and "called out" by others. The misdeeds of the notable have their formalized, public, non-apology apologies. These are domestic corrections. Whether by design, oversight, or mere lack of ambition, they leave the world mostly untouched.

I am no rebel in this. I meet my penchant for ice cream with a sterner resolve to go running. I journal my diet and receive my computer-generated course of penitential progress (my insurance plan's health coach, this world's confessor, aids me). I scour my words for unconscious expressions of bias and privilege and lament what I leave for others to discover. I apologize swiftly and deferentially for the hundred impositions I create. I read about the polar ice caps, then time my showers and cut back on beef. The Grand Inquisitor didn't anticipate the invention of the Fitbit, but it works. The honeybees will all be dead and gone before my glucose gets out of hand.

The irony is that while we are by turns indulgent and censorious, remorseful and defiant, self-improving and deft with rationalization, we are not accustomed to forgiveness, to true, full, unconditional pardon. Small sins get small grace. And just as God's judgment, as Christians hear it, is vastly more exacting and frightening than anything we can invent for ourselves, God's forgiveness is massively more gratuitous than anything

> God's forgiveness is massively more gratuitous than anything we rationally imagine receiving, utterly disproportionate to our own capacity for remorse, trust, or amendment.

we rationally imagine receiving, and utterly disproportionate to our own capacity for remorse, trust, or amendment.

Breakthrough

The communal, verbal act of confession can't help but retain some startling grandeur in this world. Whether it is one individual confessing to another or a whole assembly confessing together, the very act of utterance distinguishes this practice from the many internal sortings and accountings we are invited to make of our words and deeds. "In confession the break-through to community takes place," German theologian Dietrich Bonhoeffer says. "Sin demands to have a man to himself," but in confession "the fellowship bears the sins of the brother."[9] A sin named out loud and offered up to the ministry of the church is no longer an individual problem but a communal one.

Verbalizing a sin is both difficult and liberating. As a monastic liturgy for end-of-the-day prayer begins, "I have sinned by my fault, by my own fault, by my own most grievous fault." And however we say or mean it, it is an ironclad exclusion of the non-apology apology. Where excuse and mitigation are the necessary currency for moral life in our world—"the woman whom you gave to be with me, she gave me the fruit"—we still manage to keep them out of our verbal formulas for confession. It may feel hyperbolic, it may even *be* hyperbolic in a given instance, but the subjective hyperbole reveals the objective reality that our faults, like ourselves, can stretch almost to infinity. "You must all become something different from what you are now and act in a different way, no matter who you are now and what you do," Luther writes. "You may be as great, wise, powerful, and holy as you could want, but here no one is righteous."[10]

In the practice of this holy possession, if nowhere else in the world, our mitigations and half-measures and projects of personal improvement count for nothing. The forgiveness of one, each, and all requires no more or less generosity on God's part. That is a radical idea. To forgive the sins of a penitent but hopeless addict, or a person poisoned by lead in childhood, or an impulsive and anxious person whose biology has been permanently altered by the trauma of poverty is a dreadful thing. It can only be done while also proclaiming, yet more dreadfully, God's sure judgment and promised forgiveness to all who create and profit from the addiction, or collaborated in the poisoning, or created the poverty. We are stuck here together, and however privileged or miserable now, we will all be Adam together in the end.

Thus, even this most domestic holy possession has political and social significance. It does not ration or assign accountability and release, but accepts all of the former and an equal measure of the latter. It sets free those whom law and shame seek to keep bound, and it binds those whom power and privilege seek to keep free. It can be a liturgical and sacramental frame for communal discernment, action, and confronting destruction. Confessional services, once common among Protestants, and penitential processions, still practiced among Catholics, do this, however indirectly. In its own household and in the public street, the church offers a more urgent accountability and a more generous reconciliation than any political movement can.

Coming Home

Jesus's story about the father and his two sons (Luke 15:11–32) has never, as far as I'm concerned, been surpassed as an illustration of this generosity and reconciliation. The one son asks for his inheritance early, then goes off to "a distant country" where he squanders it in dissolute living. He ends up tending pigs and yearning to eat their food. Then he "came to himself"; he remembers that his father's hired hands have bread to eat, and he hatches a plan: "I will get up and go to my father, and I will say to him, 'Father, I have sinned against heaven and before you; I am no longer worthy to be called your son; treat me like one of your hired hands.'"

Self-talk is not good or admirable in the Gospels. We can read the son's words as the making of a speech for the sake of food rather than a sounding of his soul to be healed.

And yet he ends up deprived even of his chance to talk his way back into the outer circle of his former home. His father sees him far off, and "filled with compassion" he runs to embrace and kiss him. He cuts off the son's speech halfway through and instructs the slaves of the household to bring out the best robe, a ring, and sandals, and calls for a feast to be set, "for this son of mine was dead and is alive again; he was lost and is found."

The other son, who stayed and was faithful, stands aloof and angry. He upbraids his pleading father for never throwing a party for him and his friends, yet "when this son of yours came back, who has devoured your property with prostitutes, you killed the fatted calf for him." The father assures him of his perfect love, and insists, "We had to celebrate and rejoice, because this brother of yours was dead and has come back to life; he was lost and has been found."

In this story I've come to see a reversal of the expulsion from Eden. It's not as majestic and awe-inspiring as our parallels of tree and cross, Adam and Christ, but it is just as psychologically astute. The insinuation of the serpent is countered by the unnecessary self-talk of the son. The son, who has been rendered nearly naked by poverty, is clothed by his father not for shame but for honor, just as God's first act of grace after the Fall was to stitch proper clothing for the man and the woman. The sustenance that the son tries to scrape from the swineherd's cursed earth is given as a free gift by the father. The rhetoric of alienation is waved away by the father. The one who is "not worthy to be called your son" is "this son of mine"; the one who is castigated as "this son of *yours*" by his brother is remembered as "this brother of *yours*" by his father. The story has no penance except pain. The younger son feels pangs of hunger; the older son feels the wounds of resentment; the father feels bereft. As God's own Adam did, his child rejects him and seizes what he could have had forever as a gift. The death of a family separation is at the cusp of being undone.

In light of the story, the haggling that Christians have engaged in over the purity of the sinner's motive, the form of her verbal act, or the gesture of forgiveness offered by the confessor, however profound, seems rather beside the point. The son's motives are dubious and his words incomplete. The father's gifts of a robe and a ring are more lavish than the imposition of hands or the draping with the stole.

There's nothing miraculous in the story. A parent's disproportionate love for any child was not a concept that Jesus needed to press home to his hearers, then or now. All the same, the parable ends in a cliffhanger. Will the older son come to the party for his wastrel sibling or stand aloof? Will he accept reconciliation, and the mending of the estrangement he himself has caused, on his father's outrageous terms? Or, standing on his dignity and demanding more than reconciliation, will he end up accepting less?

The suspense of the parable is the suspense, for all of us, in this particular holy possession. Do we actually want to be reconciled to ourselves, each other, the world, and God? Do we want the cigarette to be stubbed out and all the neurons healed, the slaves set free, the dead come back, the ill-gotten gains distributed as any had need? If we do, however shaky, hypothetical, or delusional our desire, however steadfastly our brains and hearts and hands and streets await the rush of relapse, the promise is present too. And in that presence, the seeds of a new garden are sown, and the flaming sword against our homecoming is quenched.

The power of the keys—this holy possession, this sore thumb of a Christian act in a world that rations responsibility and pardon so carefully and trivially—is and can still be a glorious, solemn divestment from the world's death. When we accept the world's evil without qualification and God's grace without limit, it is a witness against the compulsion that leashes us so close to that tree, and a promise of reunion—beyond the cages we make for ourselves and each other—around it again.

Chapter 5

MINISTRY

Expatriates from the Kingdom of Usefulness

Bishop: *Before almighty God,*
to whom you must give account,
and in the presence of this assembly, I ask:
Will you assume this office,
believing that the church's call is God's call
to the ministry of word and sacrament?
Ordinand: *I will, and I ask God to help me.*
—Evangelical Lutheran Worship

Apostle to the North Side

I had come to her for confirmation. I had watched Reverend Linda Packard, and many other clergy, handle the holy materials of midweek Eucharist with love, give her attention lavishly to us needy, ruined sinners at the Tuesday-night Mass, and improvise little homilies on a saint or a text, her thumb marking the page in the prayer book where the liturgy would resume when she was done. I wanted to do those things, and I wanted her to overcome my doubts that I should.

Sitting in her office, I unburdened myself. "I just don't know whether I would do more good as a pastor than I would as a scholar, or a journalist—"

"You need to be prepared to do nobody any good at all," she told me. This is not what I had expected. It stung the breath out of me for a moment. But it was what I needed. "I used to keep thank-you notes," she said.

Years later, when she retired, I came back to pay my respects and thank her for the counsel she gave me in that moment. She remembered the meeting but not the advice. She laughed out loud at the story. "That must have been the Holy Spirit, because I would never say that." I can't look up at my own corkboard of thank-you notes without remembering her, that conversation, and all the good I had to be prepared not to do.

As we've seen with the words, water, meal, and the movement of pardon, the holy possession of ministry begins with something stubbornly ordinary: people. They are not necessarily, or even usually, terribly impressive. They are not even necessarily gifted at being Christians. And these rather ordinary people are placed in a role that is conspicuous less for what it has than what it lacks. Power, status, charisma, and deep learning are hardly unknown among clergy, but they are not the norm. A desire to do good and be useful is more typical, and typically frustrated.

A lot of us, I would later learn, are expatriates from the kingdom of usefulness who cherish their tokens of the old country. Susan was a concert violinist who played Mozart's *Laudamus Te* on Easter. Ruth was an appellate lawyer who composed her sermons and liturgical books with the detail of a legal brief. Dan was a judge in Chicago for many years and handled canonical proceedings for the Archdiocese. The deacon who helped bury my grandmother came from his job at the mechanic's shop, trying discreetly to rub the smudge of his other vocation from his hands.

In those days when I was visiting Linda's church, I assumed I was useful. I administered mentoring programs in Chicago Public Schools. Then a sophomore in a brutalized neighborhood, whose mother and siblings had been killed in a car crash when she was five, told me the only person she looked up to was God. "He's the only one who can make this all right," she told me. On the way home I resolved to update my passport and apply for my visa.

What awaits you when you arrive in ministry is a mystery. Examples of leadership in the Scriptures are not encouraging. The roles are many—prophet, priest, apostle, deacon, elder, evangelist, bishop—but the results converge in uncanny ways:

1. You get killed. This is a frequent outcome for Old Testament prophets and New Testament apostles alike.
2. You get rejected or, worse, ignored. Your words are unwelcome, unbearable, or simply evidence that you're too snobby or fanatical to be trusted. If you read Amos or certain passages of Paul's letters, it's not hard to see how this would happen.
3. You are heeded, but with unpredictable or unwelcome results. This is what happens to Jonah, who preached the destruction of Nineveh and then saw, to his humiliation, that the repentance of the people averted the promised disaster.

4. You simply fail. Prophets court favor with bad kings and priests play footsie with strange gods. Aaron gives the people, who are desperate for God's presence, a golden calf to worship. Judas betrays Jesus.

Jesus tells his inner circle that they'll be unheeded or hounded and killed, that many will fall away, that false believers and false prophets will always be on hand. And, to make matters worse, he insists on depriving us of the comforts of status and authority that make the burdens and dangers of leadership more bearable. He warns us that we'll be tempted to be exacting where freedom must prevail and hypocritical where obedience is needed. He tells us that the only greatness in his community will be that of service. Persecution must be accepted as something due to the disciples of an executed master. Rejection must be met not with a new tactic of compulsion but with a trip up the road to the next town.

On this rickety platform we have constructed optimistic theologies and images of ministry, which we maintain against bitter experience from the earliest days. Bishops and churches buckle under Roman persecution. They chase after bad bargains with hostile powers. They fixate on one part of Christian faith or life to the detriment of the rest. They answer questions no one asked. My Danish ancestry drew me to Ansgar (801–865 AD), first bishop of Hamburg, patron saint of Denmark and "apostle to the North." When I read the account of his life, I learned that he was extraordinarily humble and generous. I also learned that his Scandinavian missions all died out, and his cathedral was burned down in his lifetime. He even managed to fail at martyrdom, that heroic self-offering that covers all other failures. Given that he traveled extensively in Viking-infested lands, martyrdom shouldn't have exactly been rocket science.

There is, of course, much more to it than betrayal and failure, abandoned missions and nations filled with sullen half-believers. There were also those leaders who held fast, who swayed multitudes, who won and held little worlds for faith. But both triumph and tragedy are tricks of retrospect. Augustine spent his life in service to the church, navigating many crises and in his spare time writing some of the foundational texts of Western theology. But he died at a moment that looked like the end of Roman Christian North Africa. It was the same for Ansgar. When pressed by his companions about rumors of miracles, he replied that if he were worthy of such good favor from God, he would ask only that God in his grace would make him a good man. The ends, good or bad, are not in your hand. You have to be prepared to do nobody any good at all.

Administering the Frontier

Why does anybody, clergy or people, put up with ministry, much less treat it as a holy possession? Part of the answer is that *some-*

body has to do it. The holy possessions imply a person entrusted with handling and enacting them. Someone must do the proclaiming, the baptizing, the breaking of bread, the loosing and binding of sins for the rest, and in turn have those things done for him or herself. "What would happen," Luther asked, "if everyone wanted to speak or administer, and no one wanted to give way to the other?"[1]

But it's not just necessity that makes the calling and ordaining of ministers a holy possession, a blessing for Christians and a public sign of their presence in the world. Leadership in the Christian community does something essential. But in this age of scandal and irrelevance, what exactly is that something? What has it ever been?

The New Testament is vague on church structures, perhaps reflecting overlapping networks of prophets, apostles, and deacons in the early churches. Before long, the titles of "prophet" and "apostle" fell out of regular use in the church (though some shadows of the functions would remain, and they would make resurgences wherever the official structures of the church became ossified). In Christian societies, the offices came to reflect different roles in the social body. Clerical power mirrored civil power. Their roles were specified and distinguished from each other, but both were understood as being established by God in their own realms for their own necessary purposes. Clergy were entitled to dignities and prerogatives that reflected worldly, secular hierarchies.

Luther and most of the Reformers sought to center ministry more narrowly on preaching the Word and administering the sacraments, "administering" being an unlovely word we've been stuck with a long time now. They eliminated and renamed some offices (I'm not sure what we gained by calling bishops "superintendents," but there you go) and diminished their mythos. The priest was no longer the person uniquely capable of turning the wine into blood; he was just the person appointed to do so on behalf of the whole assembly. But looking back from the present day, the differences between Christian traditions in the theory and practice of leadership are rather dwarfed by the enduring similarities.

When I consider this history—of which my own vocation is very much a part—in light of Jesus's commands and warnings, it seems an awful lot like a big mistake. Those people summoned to leadership in the Christian community were to imitate the authorities of the world only by utterly inverting them. In Matthew's Gospel, every sin for which Jesus condemned contemporary leaders ("But woe to you, scribes and Pharisees, hypocrites!") is one we made customary before the first Christian millennium was out.

Early on, the Christian community was faced with the problem of leaders who had denied the faith and handed over the sacred texts under persecution. We concluded that however badly those people failed, the grace they administered (there's not a better way to put it, in this light) was still valid. Baptism still forgives sin; Eucharist still unites the faithful with Christ; ordination still makes a real priest. This says something true and beautiful about how God chooses to relate to a hopelessly imperfect human community.

But it says something rather dark about the practice of authority among ourselves. Goodness in a bishop was nice to have but not required; obedience to that bishop was mandatory. We clergy could convince ourselves that the obedience was not for the benefit of us, the shepherds, but rather for the sake of the sheep. But the scribes Jesus condemns would have said the same thing. You can't plead your good motives when the religious control you exercise treats your motives as irrelevant.

Because God is generous and because God's people are resourceful, there was a blessing in this bureaucracy of grace. The very un-Jesus-like structures of authority we created gave space and freedom for compelling experiments in faith and life. Monastic orders, scholastic theology, and aesthetic innovations all had a chance to win approval, or at least benign neglect, in that space. Good leaders built important, enduring institutions. An official clergy, however contrary to the spirit of Jesus's teachings on authority, allowed the words of Jesus an echo in the councils of power that they wouldn't otherwise have had.

The habits of public deference to clergy in America lingered until well into the last century. A man—and then it was always a man, and typically white—who occupied a prominent pulpit or office could admonish and encourage America from the greater gravity of that ecclesial space.

This public deference is over. Church leaders prominent enough to play a role in politics today are not mediators of a transcendent religious tradition, but brokers of a voting bloc. They are fully assimilated into our secular culture, however aggressively Christian their branding.

For the rest of us, Christian ministry in a secular society has become an inescapably hybrid practice. It plants us on several margins at once. The minister resides on the frontier between a past centered on the Christian story and an increasingly centerless present. She stands at the point of contact between the exemplary, even imaginary Christian life her people aspire—or at least *want* to aspire—to live, and the ruthlessly demanding ambiguities of the world in which they do live. She speaks an authoritative Word into a world that is, with good reason, suspicious of authoritative claims. And she beckons in the opposite direction, from a contingent and ever-changing secular world into a Kingdom of God. My mentor, preaching to me at my ordination, told me we aren't called to be successful; we're called to be faithful. But it's hard to know what either success or faithfulness looks like from these frontiers. Ansgar, planted on the frontier of Christian Europe and pagan Scandinavia, and Augustine, living and dying where the Roman Empire ended, faced the same perplexity.

But the truth and the holiness of this ministry have always resided in its placelessness, its powerlessness, its marginal existence. Its holiness resides in both the desire to do great good to anyone, and the willingness to do no good at all. It is not in imitating the world's structures of power that ministry blesses the church and the world; it is by escaping them.

Genuine Authority

Wary and cynical as our world can appear, it harbors a strange and naive craving for leadership. It raises up gurus who reveal and sell hidden knowledge. It seizes on entrepreneurs who innovate and disrupt their way through the world's complex problems. It glorifies strongmen who overwhelm opposition with their force of character. Leaders get results.

Christian churches and their leaders, faced with unhappy trends, want results. So the cult of leadership has found favor among Christians who suspect a secular society of not wanting Jesus or faith or church, and of needing to be cajoled or tricked into acting as if it does. The tricks and techniques of modern leadership can even work, for a while, until they flame out in scandal, abuse, or disappointment. Gurus drift away from a concrete community to pursue a bigger, broader audience; entrepreneurs turn local innovations into business enterprises; strongmen hide their weaknesses behind authoritarian structures. These failures follow inevitably when the holy possession of ministry drifts from the margins where God plants it onto the safer ground of worldly wisdom.

In the face of scandal and failure, it is tempting to devise a spiritual reform or a new theological description of ministry to revive its essence. Surely there is some way back to that dangerous, God-haunted charisma that spread the Gospel far and wide before seminary programs and tax exemptions were ever dreamed of. Perhaps in turning away from these unworthy techniques of control, we can recover "authenticity," as if that too weren't a form of branding. Or a fresh application of zeal may do the trick. When a colleague complained about indifferent parishioners to John Vianney, Roman Catholic patron of parish pastors, he asked, "Have you slept on the floor?" That may be worth a shot. But his suggestion is some 150 years old. There's probably nothing new under the sun where reform of the clergy is concerned.

The holiness of this possession, like the word, the bath, the meal, and the forgiveness, is not in what it could ideally be, but in what it really already is. Dietrich Bonhoeffer, writing about Christian community, warned against a "spiritually sick need for the admiration of men, for the establishment of visible human authority." This need, whether it is fulfilled with tactics borrowed from a corporate leadership manual or a frantic redoubling of pious effort, flourishes "because *the genuine authority of service appears to be so unimpressive*."[2] If leadership as

The holiness of this possession, like the word, the bath, the meal, and the forgiveness, is not in what it could ideally be, but in what it really already is.

we see it represented in the world today cultivates power without responsibility, leadership in the Christian community cultivates responsibility without power. It is a tool for surrendering and dispersing the goods we are elsewhere taught to hoard for ourselves.

The first and striking thing about ministry among Christians is how purely *representative* it can be. A person who says "the body of Christ, given for you" or "I forgive your sins" need not believe them in the moment, because they are not her words. They are words in her custody, so to say—committed to her care by the people of God for the sake of all—but they do not spring from her genius, nor do they depend on her power to make them plausible or intelligible.

This custody (or stewardship, to use a biblical term) may take many forms. But it is central to Christian life because we are not a movement of heroically spiritual individualists who are equipped to examine, absolve, and preach to ourselves. The external Word is the gift, freely offered to the whole Creation but commended to each of us by the narrow gates of our own senses. It's not something in a book or a screen but in the lively presence of another. God orders this gift to our good, but it partakes of all the contingency and fragility that we feel in our own lives, contingency and fragility that are cruelly obscured by the frictionless pretensions of our world. While the abusive or corrupt cleric is a killer of faith and souls, the merely lazy, confused, or disheartened cleric may be a miraculous witness to God's grace. He is there, heaving grace into the pews or plush seats by the bushel.

"We have this treasure in clay jars," Paul the Apostle tells the church in Corinth. I remind myself that I am bearing a treasure when my vestments are spotty and drab. And when I'm feeling electric, I try to remember that I'm still just a clay vessel. *Here's your jar, Christian. You shouldn't break it, but neither can you buy its contents.*

This representative function is also the easily obscured blessing in honorific titles and clerical garb. Neither a costume nor a uniform, it is the visible sign of a demand placed on the minister to preach, teach, bless, and forgive anyone who asks. Fulfill it well or poorly, the demand itself is simply objective and unwavering.

More strangely, ministry confers blessing and liberation in its *weakness*. This is not necessarily the weakness of the meek and persecuted who are blessed in the words of Jesus. Rather, it is weakness in fact, weakness as a condition rather than a passing circumstance. People can literally stand up while we're talking, walk out, and never come back (ask me how I know!). Hurling a threat of excommunication and hell after them is, whatever else, inevitably an expression of resentment at their exercise of freedom. A friend with no acquaintance with church asked me how we fund ourselves. He was astonished to learn that we pass a plate, and whatever we get, we get. This comes home in poignant ways, when housing values collapse or job losses hit and the church's ministries (and salaries) share the downturn. Or, more discouragingly, when the one preaching to the community says things that the community doesn't want to hear. An old Chicago pastor told me that whenever he preached to his predominantly white church about welcoming their new black neighbors, the offering would plummet. "The Catholic priest and I used to compare how many bottle caps we got in the offering" instead of money, he said.

We see this more clearly now that we have lost all of our official power to compel, but it has always been true. Ambrose, the story goes, turned Emperor Theodosius away from the church in Milan because Theodosius had impulsively ordered a massacre and needed to do penance. It would not have been impossible for Theodosius to have had Ambrose killed and his church razed. And if Ambrose had wielded a different kind of authority than what Bonhoeffer called the authority of service—which looks so unimpressive, holds no cards, and travels unarmed—the emperor probably would have.

To take a more homely example, a person who agrees to an end-user service agreement for Spotify is giving that service more intimate access to her life than she is likely to give me in a decade of Sunday pew occupancy. Considering the limits of my repertoire and the unevenness of my sound quality, I can't complain about this. We are a society of raw materials, waiting to be targeted, mined, and aggregated, not to mention instructed, employed, indebted, and perhaps incarcerated, all at a profit. It is only rational, in every case, to make our best bargains and minimize our exposure to risk. But when we encounter the ministry of the church, whether in a hospital room, in a pastor's study, or around the altar, something very different happens. A door opens from the inside that can't be pried open by any kind of compulsion. When we encounter this holy possession, we don't experience our freedom as something that can be surrendered under duress or exchanged for value. We encounter our freedom as something that can only be freely offered.

Still, even though ministry is a modest stewardship, and marked by weakness, it is an act of *resistance* in its marginality. It is the location at all those margins—between past and present, ideal and actual, authority and skepticism, the Kingdom of God and the kingdoms of this world—that gives Christian ministry its continuing power to bless and sanctify the church. When Pope Francis says that clergy should have "the odor of sheep,"[3] he's not just indulging in populist color, but suggesting that leaders must stand where the people stand and know what the people know, if only to be able to point them beyond it.

If ministers weren't an anachronism, we would have nothing to say to the world; if we weren't fully embedded in this world, we would have no reason to speak in the first place. If we were not fully accountable to the infinite demands and infinite grace of God in Christ, we would be busybodies and charlatans. But if we were not also accountable to the hesitations and demurrals of our moment in history, we would be daydreamers and perfectionists. If we abandon the idea of God's kingdom, we lose the power to fight the world's evils and injustices; if we abandon the world, we lose the reason for fighting, and all that might be protected and nurtured by fighting. To leave the margin is to fail, and to stay there is to be absurd. But Christianity is absurd, so there we are. The great stone edifice is too cold and dingy for an office, so pastor and parishioner meet over five-dollar coffee to describe a world without want or need. Sunday's Gospel is a promise of easy burdens and rest for all who labor; Monday is a side hustle to pay off student loans from seminary. You were not called to be exemplary; you were called to be faithful.

If we abandon the world, we lose the reason for fighting, and all that might be protected and nurtured by fighting. To leave the margin is to fail, and to stay there is to be absurd. But Christianity is absurd, so there we are.

Prince of the Apostles

The epilogue of the Gospel of John tells us that, after Jesus had risen from the dead and commissioned his friends to forgive or retain sins in his name, Peter decided to go back to fishing. The others followed him. Peter would eventually be honored with the title "Prince of the Apostles," an epithet I can only understand by virtue of its absurdity. Jesus calls him Rock in his faith and Satan in his refusal to accept that the Messiah will suffer. He's so zealous that he cuts a guy's ear off to protect Jesus, and then so frightened that he denies knowing Jesus at all. And then when the nascent Jesus Movement is cut loose in the world, he goes back to the little place in the Roman imperial economic system he knows he can occupy, on the piece of earth he knows best, doing the useful thing he knows how to do. So do all the rest. Left by Jesus on the frontier, Jesus's friends go home.

But, in the sort of dramatic irony for which the Scriptures are famous, their nets come up empty. Jesus, hidden from their recognition, tells them to cast on the other side of the boat, which yields a massive haul. On the shore, Jesus puts Peter through an unforgettable catechism: "Simon, son of John, do you love me more than these?" he asks him three times, echoing Peter's three denials, to the point of wounding him. After Peter answers yes each time, Jesus tells him to feed his sheep. Then Jesus foretells Peter's crucifixion. To put it in Bonhoeffer's terms, Jesus calls Peter to exercise the utterly unimpressive authority of service.

This is the moment on which leadership in the Christian community depends. Jesus establishes this strange, under-credentialed, un-located, unequipped role to deny and defy the people and ideas who would be happy to assimilate or eliminate it. But you can't assimilate what's useless, and you can't eliminate what's absurd. Like the bathing, the meal, and the loosing of infinite sin, this story—and its distant repetition in the calling and consecrating of ministers through all the years that follow—marks out a space that can't be conquered by any empire.

Chapter 6

PRAYER, PRAISE, AND WORSHIP

Redeeming Work

Officiant: *O Lord, open thou our lips.*

People: *And our mouth shall show forth thy praise.*

—The Book of Common Prayer

Candles in Daylight

Lila, the narrator of Marilynne Robinson's 2014 novel, is a religious "none" long before the term was invented. Working constantly to survive and wholly innocent of religion, she wanders into a church and poses a pointed question: "Why did they waste candles on daylight?" There is a luxury involved in worshiping. It is unaccountable from the standpoint of the need and anxiety of the world in which worship happens. "There was no need for any of it," she continues.

> The days came and went on their own, without any praying about it. And still, everywhere, meetings and revivals, people seeing the light. Finding comfort where there was no comfort, just an old man saying something he'd said so many times he probably didn't hear it himself.[1]

With this sixth marker on our itinerary of Christian practice—"prayer, public praise, and worship"—we make a kind of progress.[2] We have traveled from the impossible—in the counting of sparrows, the drowning of human distinctions, the sharing of Christ's body and blood, the forgiveness of eternal and ineradicable sin—to the absurd, in setting apart ministers to do these things. And now we arrive at mere waste, at candles burning in daylight.

When Israel came out of exile in Babylon, its numbers and its implements for worship were catalogued in numbing specificity. Whole chapters of nothing but accounting. One at a time they are burdensome. But taken together they become hypnotic in their solicitude for detail. Of the Benjaminites, Scripture says, 956 remained in Jerusalem after the exile. It was important to the chroniclers to get this right, to lose nothing more to a world that had destroyed so much, and to add nothing to a world already so crammed with legends.

Israel brought home thirty gold basins and a thousand of silver; twenty-nine knives and thirty gold bowls—all taken back from Nebuchadnezzar, who had seized them for his own gods. The act of memory is the critical thing. How precious each silver basin must have been when it had been ripped out of its place and dedicated to some other god, only to be brought back as a seed for a new place of worship.

The Bible's attention to detail poses a problem. It is lavish where reasonable people (i.e., us) are inclined to be economical. It expands where we might expect it to summarize. It demands precise memory where venerable legend might be more useful. It uses a great deal of parchment when a small amount might suffice. It sets out candles in daylight.

And this lavishness repeats a problem with worship itself. It is a puzzle. It consumes vast amounts of time, attention, and resources that could be used for something more obviously productive. It's not obvious what this expenditure *does.*

That's not to say it does nothing. Of all the holy possessions, this is the most common and democratic. It's hard to find Christians without finding prayers, psalms, songs, candles, and incense being heaved outward and upward. It is a possession held and practiced in such a variety of ways that it can be hard to sense any unity connecting the silence of the Carthusian monk and the ecstasy of the Pentecostal praise band. But it is all a shared sacrifice offered to the God who calls us through the Word, washes us in baptism, feeds us at the table, forgives our sins, and raises up leaders to see that all of this is done. If it appears, even to us at times, to be a waste, it is a liberating and necessary waste.

The People's Work

Worship is older than the Bible, maybe as old as humanity itself. In traditional religious societies, worship organizes life. It marks out space and time, distinguishes the sacred from the ordinary, preserves collective memories, and reinforces social relationships. It enacts a great cosmic exchange, with humans offering up animals, incense, or words to ensure divine favor coming down.

Looking down from the rooftop deck of modernity, the actions humans have used to do all these things can appear arbitrary, inexplicable, or even horrifying. Human sacrifice, to pick only the most obvious example, is not uncommon in the history of religion. The command to turn away from child sacrifice, and the apparent temptation to slide back to it, is an ongoing theme in the Old Testament. Throughout the Bible, rituals of worship are retrofitted to serve only God.

The work, however, is an enduring fact of all worship. The whole worshiping world is united in the time and effort it devotes to this extravagant thing. When I march through my morning psalms and fold my hands for my ten-thousandth recitation of the Lord's Prayer, I don't feel especially connected to Noah making a burnt offering of every clean bird and animal. I blanch at the thought of drawing the knife over and over. But the prophet Hosea instructs the people, when their sin is forgiven, to say, "We will offer the bulls of our lips."[3] So there we are, Noah and I, putting our shoulders to the wheel of prayer.

Christians borrowed homely Greek words for their shared offering of prayer and thanksgiving. They called it *leitourgia*, meaning "people's work." It's the root of the rarified English word "liturgy." The people who gathered for this work were called an *ekklesia*, a local assembly that could be convened for anything from making public decisions to digging a latrine.

Early Christians packed vast meanings into these unassuming terms. In their work they prayed the simple but expansive prayer

Jesus taught, calling God "Father," sanctifying God's name, appealing for the doing of God's will and the coming of God's kingdom. The *Didache*, an early Christian text, imagines all of Christ's people, now scattered in their worship, being gathered into one great assembly at the end of the age. It puts a finer point on Jesus's prayer: "May grace come and may this world pass away."[4]

Yet alongside these ambitious petitions were prayers for modest daily needs: for daily bread, for mutual forgiveness of sins and debts, for preservation from trials, for the welfare of rulers and recovery from illness. There was a daily and weekly rhythm, with Christians gathering at morning and evening as the bells of Roman cities rang, and each week for the sacramental meal. Mid-day prayers and days of fasting united the dispersed assembly in a shared practice.

From the beginning, the people's work had two enduring purposes in seeming tension with each other: We pray for the needs of this world, and we pray for the coming of the Kingdom of God.

I'm still not sure what effect these people intended when they assembled for their work. When they prayed "Thy kingdom come" or "May grace come and may this world pass away," were these words meant to hasten the completion of the Messianic age, shouts to nudge the wicked world's mountain slope toward an avalanche? Or were those words a way of transporting themselves to that end, to the kingdom, to begin to dwell there as a present reality even in the midst of a not-fully-redeemed world, however long the fullness tarried in coming? Does prayer change the world's timeline, or shift the course of an illness? Or does prayer change us?

For many spiritually ambitious Christians, as well as for theologians, the most important purpose of prayer and worship was to move those who pray. But instead of praying ourselves *forward* in time, to an expected boundary between this world and the world of grace, we prayed *upward*, from worldly life to the transcendence and blessedness of God. Pseudo-Dionysius described prayer as preparation of the soul for union with God, a movement as if by a "shining chain" that appears to pull God toward us when in fact it is lifting us toward God.[5] Prayer fits us for God by purifying thought and desire and training them on divine things.

But prayers for more ordinary purposes flourished, too. People could pray for anything they wanted, and they could want absolutely anything. As long as the need wasn't sinful, and as long as it was sought with the motive of eternal blessedness, it was approved.[6] Our motives are vague and inconstant, but our needs are enduring, so rituals and prayers proliferated.

So, alone or together, for good reasons and bad, Christians have prayed and worshiped for the soul's blessedness and the body's needs, asking "forgive

So, alone or together, for good reasons and bad, Christians have prayed and worshiped for the soul's blessedness and the body's needs, asking "forgive us our sins" and "give us this day our daily bread."

us our sins" and "give us this day our daily bread." When Luther and the other Reformers came along, they sought to clarify the purposes of worship. They distinguished between "sacrament," which is God's gracious gift to us, and "sacrifice," which is our grateful response. Prayer can't lift our souls to heaven because no human work can accomplish that. But prayer and praise could and must be used as a way to give thanks for the grace by which God lifts us to heaven, and to appeal for God's help in all our daily needs. "In fact, God's kingdom comes on its own without our prayer," Luther writes in his Small Catechism, "but we ask in this prayer that it may also come to us."[7]

There is by now no counting of the books of prayers, hymns, liturgical orders, and devotions made by Christians to recall themselves to their peculiar work. None of it is truly wasted. The words of prayer, praise, and thanksgiving, insubstantial as they are and fragile as their parchment records may be, have outlived every exile. The slurry of motives behind them, from years of purgatory remitted to relief from the plague to union with God to incantations for prosperity, are, if anything, a witness to the ambition of the people's work and its endurance through endless changes of language, culture, and historical circumstance. The small remains of Augustine's cathedral languish unrestored today, but his plea still stands: "My soul is like a house, small for you to enter, but I pray you to enlarge it. It is in ruins, but I ask you to remake it."[8]

The Power of Prayer

So prayer and worship are the people's work, aimed at blessedness and sustenance, and enduring through time at least for the sake of the beauty and creativity they have inspired. But does this people's work actually . . . work? Does it confer blessing or answer bodily needs?

If prayer for human needs has some effect, it seems that we should be able to discern it. Ever since Francis Galton, a nineteenth-century English statistician, found no extra longevity among monarchs—the most prayed-for class—there have been attempts to find a prayer effect in the world. Skeptics and believers alike have made this search, which makes prayer into a kind of treatment, discoverable in a double-blind test of the soul. Some modern believers like to talk about the "power of prayer," running parallel to the power of medicine (or politics, or economics), and perhaps even a substitute for it. But the search has been, at best, frustratingly inconclusive. Miraculous healings correlated with prayer are not unknown; the world may be more resistant to our rational, scientific ways of knowing it than we can say or even guess. But whenever we've tried to chase God out of the thicket of life's causes by making prayer into a treatment and testing its effects, God has not obliged.

On the other hand, if it's hard to find an effect of prayer in the world, there is some evidence that prayer and worship do something in us. Repetitive prayer practices have been found to contribute to mental and physical well-being and even to affect the operation of the brain. If you're trying to maintain memory or control anxiety, certain kinds of prayer seem to help.[9] Practices that not long ago would have been firmly located in the world of religion have become accepted as therapy. And participation in public religious services seems to correlate with lots of good things, even if it's not clear exactly why, as does singing in a group (something we may not emphasize enough as we market our faith to a skeptical world).

But there are obvious problems with even the most optimistic studies of prayer. For one thing, no empirical method can assess the effectiveness of prayer in helping a soul to reach blessedness. If there is a "shining chain" along which prayer can move us, we don't know in a scientifically meaningful way where it leads or from whence it hangs. For another, the study of prayer doesn't make or discover any claims for Christian practices specifically. The rosary seems to do some good, but nothing more or different than Buddhist meditation does. Christians aren't the only people who gather for healthful group singing or emotionally hygienic bonds of fellowship. Prayer can be won back from the secular world only, it seems, by translating it into secular terms—by making it into pure technique. Leave the bowls in Babylon and make some new ones. They'll work just as well.

Worse, not only are we tempted to diminish prayer to the terms made available to us by our age and culture, but we can end up enlisting our practices in support of fundamentally secular ends. "Pray the Rosary for America," a parish church will invite passersby, which is something like the opposite of praying "Thy kingdom come." Meditate to reduce your health care costs and become a better worker. Say the prayer of Jabez every day to get rich. May grace hold off a while; let this world remain.

The actual history of prayer, praise, and thanksgiving is not even remotely so domesticated. Its effects are too subtle and strange to pin down with a double-blind study or an MRI. That is not to evade the question. I can't help but ask myself what, exactly, I'm doing when I recite the Lord's Prayer each day, ritually, without a thought that the kingdom will come soon or late, to the world or to me; or when I stand at the head of the assembly and offer petitions for leaders, for the sick, or for our dying planet. If the "power of prayer" isn't something we can lock into a category we call "spirituality," if it isn't a sort of alternative medicine, perhaps it's shaping the world in other, more literal, more troublesome ways.

Redeeming Work

To call prayer and worship among Christians "the people's work" is to make a startling and significant claim in our world. Work, after all, is something most of us are obliged to understand. To live is to work, for most human beings, ever since the Garden.

We've been driven toward industry by need on the one hand and by a curious delight in making things on the other.

But in our moment in history, work is different. It has lost any natural structure. Work is even losing its cultural structure. The movement from farms to factories and offices erased the rhythm of the seasons. The invention of electricity erased the distinction between day and night. Modern communication and information technologies have erased the distinction between home and workplace for many people. Nations—or, in a revealing synecdoche, "economies"—are urged by our sages to embrace "flexible labor markets," which sounds good until you try to visualize who is being flexed. Labor is no longer a human thing, but a commodity that can be sliced and allocated and arranged in any configuration an employer requires. This flexibility is perfectly compatible with high rates of unemployment, underemployment, and informal work. It feeds on them. The low-income service worker is an excellent candidate for doing some Uber driving on the side.

At the same time, work has become an ideology. Work is an end in itself. We get habituated to it from a young age, with education and, increasingly, extracurricular activities having the shape of work. They prepare us for life in the "labor force"—another phrase that sounds sinister once you try to visualize it—by cultivating marketable skills and office-ready qualities of character. Perhaps most importantly, they teach us how to do the things the world seems to demand of us. Political, ideological, and economic elite groups are hostile to retirement programs and public pensions, deeply resistant to paid parental leave, and suspicious of people who can't earn enough by selling their labor to get by. We exist to produce. Walter Brueggemann calls all of this a "market ideology" that depends on "the generation of needs and desires that will leave us endlessly 'rest-less,' inadequate, unfulfilled, and in pursuit of that which may satiate desire."[10] This ideology, which can fairly be called the worship of a god, doesn't work for everyone, so we have incarceration, chemical dependency, and various kinds of official obsolescence. And this ideology doesn't exclude leisure, which is constantly available in trivial little packets to anyone with a smartphone.

The ideology of work seems strong enough to endure even the disappearance of whole categories of jobs to automation. Today's Uber-driving retail worker can be made redundant tomorrow by automated home deliveries and driverless cars; and yet the loss of income and self-worth that this transformation will inflict on individuals and communities will be widely regarded as their fault, or the fault of some other dispossessed group. We really have become, to a large degree, what we are paid to do. We don't know what we'll be without it.

Like each of the holy possessions we've explored, the grandiose luxury of worship can be impoverished into a form that is more useful. Churches can make worship yet another task, or else make it into a spectacle for us to consume. We know how to be busy, and we know how to be entertained. When we experience the people's work as a holy possession, however, we are doing something different. We are stepping outside of our culture of frantic work and restless consumption. We are stepping outside of the brutal logic of necessity and obsolescence.

Prayer and worship critique that culture, and they create an alternative to it. The people's work is a shadow work, a subversive work, even a parody of our habits and our politics. People assemble in the morning of the first day with nothing in hand to give to a God who, unlike the gods of the market ideology, needs nothing. Voices join in blurry unison where competition can have no winners. Countless thoughts, intentions, and dispositions congeal around words spoken so many times they can scarcely be said to be spoken at all, for all the visible effect they have. No one supervises or corrects the group or bends it toward the mission statement. *Lord, in your mercy, hear our prayer. We believe in one God, the Father, the Almighty.* The people's work can never be compelled, completed, or replaced.

Even in its sleepiest, most tedious performance, this is an uncanny reversal of how our world works. Wrenching so much as an hour away from our roles as workers and consumers is an act of resistance. The church at prayer takes up space in the world. It appropriates the time, attention, and concern that would otherwise be handed over without a second thought to the subtle and persuasive forces that drive so much of life. The less we assert our claims for prayer and worship as alternative medicine or self-help, the clearer this appropriation is. "Somebody prayed for me, had me on their mind / They took the time and prayed for me," a gospel song goes. In a capitalist economy, prayer is like donated labor. "I'll be praying for you" is a phrase that falls between "I'll be thinking of you" and "I'll bring over a casserole": it creates and reinforces a social bond that is deeper than the actual words and accountable only in God's ledger. Our harmonies, however clumsy, and prayers, however raggedy, are the gold and silver basins that must not be allowed to remain as adornment for Babylon's temples. They are coming home with us, even if it's only for an hour.

But this is only part of the answer to the question of how this holy possession sanctifies and blesses Christian people in the world today. After all, going to a place and singing hymns to Jesus with other Jesus enthusiasts isn't the only thing you can do with an hour snatched away from your boss and Facebook. You could make dinner for friends, or have sex, or play volleyball. None of those things turn up in GDP figures, either. The people's work is more than a withholding from the world; it is also an offering. It is not just resistance; it is creation.

Prayer and worship are supposed to form people, individually and together—not necessarily to form the preternaturally calm or infection-resistant people looked for in prayer studies, but to form people in charity and hope. The habit of prayer, ritually and communally renewed, connects the disparate moments of our lives and the scattered intentions of our hearts. It holds together the highest desires we've been taught to cherish and our stubborn reluctance to see them fulfilled. A young Augustine remembers praying, to the mockery of the ages, "Give me chastity and continence, but not yet." His ambivalence is part of the whole assembly's prayer: "May grace come, but not yet." To offer our wayward intentions and the world into which they careen all up together in the stylized and formalized language of prayer and pleading and benediction—this is perhaps the most reverently human work there is.

> The habit of prayer, ritually and communally renewed, connects the disparate moments of our lives and the scattered intentions of our hearts. It holds together the highest desires we've been taught to cherish and our stubborn reluctance to see them fulfilled.

This is the meaning of the polemical and easily misused phrase "the priesthood of all believers." It's not that each and every one of us is a religious specialist, or that all have the same roles and the same authority. Rather, it is the common human ability, called forth in the Word and empowered by baptism, to make a sacrifice of the humblest things we have to offer, starting with our words and thoughts. And it is at the same time the conviction, sealed in thanksgiving, that God accepts these prayers with perfect condescension, discerning the melody of praise in the cacophony of our divided lives.

It doesn't help the visibility of this possession that we so often hold it in a shoddy or careworn manner. But the wonder is not that people do this poorly, but that they do it at all. This is the work of anticipation, of people working together to craft an amateurish homage to the great communion that is being revealed by God. In that sense, "Thy kingdom come" really does swing us forward, together, to the event horizon of God's promises, even if we fall backward after every "Amen." The candles are the grateful and hopeful response to the miracle of daylight and the greater day to come.

It is no accident, then, that this holy possession of the church has been subject to so many restrictions, even in putatively Christian societies. And it's certainly no coincidence that the people's work is most dangerous when it takes place outside of church buildings. Eritrean refugees wall off a place for worship in "The Jungle" in Calais, France, caught between an oppressive homeland and an unwelcoming Europe. The Church beyond the Walls gathers people with and without housing, year round, in a public park in Providence, Rhode Island.

Christians transform little patches of this world into the world of grace. These patches are never so little that they don't risk foreclosure by a state that has no use for whatever they're doing. Shrewd governments have often sought to narrow the range of times, places, and manners of prayer, or to proscribe some central text in the people's work. They are not wrong to sense sedition in it, and not foolish to hedge it safely in the private space of religious enthusiasm. There's no telling what might happen when words of limitless hope waft through the seams and wounds of a society. Wherever the world is ending, you can find prayer and praise, pointing back to a time before Christians had their own protected buildings, and forward to a time when, as the song in Luke's Gospel says, God's people will be "free to worship him without fear." Candles wasted on daylight, bowls stolen back from the gods, comfort proclaimed where there is no comfort, words repeated time out of mind—all, in their rejection of mere facts and in their ferocious hope, sanctify the world twice over: once in what those who pray become, and again in what they promise the world will be.

Chapter 7

CROSS

The Beginning and the End

Only a suffering God can help.

—Dietrich Bonhoeffer

The First Day

We started our journey together in the mystery of suffering things, and that's where we conclude. We might expect the holy possessions of Christian people to deliver us to a new place, to guide us to a new achievement of insight or holiness, or to provide for us a resolution of the problems and paradoxes they bring to light. But the itinerary marked by these things is not a triumphant progress. Instead, it is a recurring encounter with Christ through the essential moments of calling, washing, eating, reconciliation, and praise.

And so Luther crowns his inventory of the church's holy possessions not with the glory of virtuous deeds or beautiful art, but "the holy possession of the sacred cross"—the suffering and persecution imposed on those who "want to have none but Christ, and no other God."[1] To ponder, and grasp, this possession is to fall back on the haunting, enduring questions of faith. How do we reconcile the unnecessary gift of existence with the absurdity of suffering? And how do we see the God of heaven and earth, above and beyond all time and space, in the person of Jesus of Nazareth?

James Weldon Johnson's poetic paraphrase of Genesis, "The Creation," offers a tale hinting at an explanation:

> And God stepped out on space,
> And he looked around and said:
> I'm lonely—
> I'll make me a world.

So God, shrouded in darkness "Blacker than a hundred midnights / Down in a cypress swamp," smiles the light into existence, shapes it into sun and moon, and flings stars into heaven. He lays down the earth and shapes its features with his footsteps. His hands and words produce seas and thunder, rainbows and animals. Still, for all the joy he takes in his abundant creation, God is lonely.

Christians aren't supposed to believe in a God who suffers loneliness. It's a problem to say that God suffers anything at all. God is self-sufficient, complete, and needing nothing. When the Scriptures show us a plaintive or changeable God, we say that God condescends to our ability to know, that God "speaks with a lisp" when the text gives him hands, nostrils, or ordinary human emotions (or, for that matter, a biological sex). Even so, loneliness is not, as far as I know, ever ascribed to God in the Scriptures. Johnson's imaginative leap crosses a real mystery in the story, and indeed in pretty much all the theologians I've read: What could have prompted such a thing as God to make such a thing as a universe, let alone us, the most febrile part of that universe?

So Johnson's lonely God sits down by the riverside, head in hands, and resolves, "I'll make me a man!" So he scooped up the clay, and "by the bank of the river / He kneeled him down," and, having smiled and clapped a universe into being, "Like a mammy bending over her baby . . . toiling over a lump of clay," made the human being in his own image, gave it the breath of life from his own lungs. "And man became a living soul. / Amen. Amen."[2] In Johnson's poem, God creates out of his own suffering, not with speech but with manual labor. The hands that spun the light into a sun thrust down into clay and carefully, deliberately, like a mammy brooding over her baby, turn the lump into a human being. As a mother broods over her child, as the child broods over the plush bear she loves, so God acts with absolute power and equal vulnerability. So God would share the world with someone who can love back, hear and speak back, know herself as a creature, and share in the task of creation.

To imagine God first as suffering loneliness, and then as creating by hand, is to gain a fresh appreciation of how the suffering we impose on each other grieves God so deeply. Christians have long understood violence as a crime against "the image of God." That's a grand phrase, but it is diminished today, when images can be endlessly reproduced. I treasure my image of Pieter Brueghel's *The Harvesters*; it is beautiful and majestic, but it is, in the age of mechanical and digital reproduction, infinitely replaceable—thank you, Walter Benjamin. What's one image or a thousand, more or less?

Handiwork is different. It's personal and particular. God plants the ear and forms the eye, as the psalm says. God enters world history, in Exodus, as the God of slaves—the people who work by hand—and not the people who give orders. Their labor had dignity even if its fruits were stolen from them. Maybe it's the hand in the clay and the breath in the nostrils, not the nature of God projected in miniature into our mind, that makes us so prized, and so apt to disappoint.

All the suffering that follows the Creation is, in one way or another, the war of clay against clay: brother against brother, men against women, Pharaoh against slaves, nation against nation. Humans were made as the coda to all life, and yet we make death for ourselves and each other, miraculous living souls so willing to dissolve and be dissolved back into the dust and the breath from which we came. The godlike power to create and delight in creation turns to perverse and monstrous purposes. God made humans, but humans make gods. King Nebuchadnezzar builds a giant idol, then threatens to heave anyone who refuses to worship it into a great fiery furnace, a kiln in reverse, to destroy their obstinate lumps of clay. Into that furnace he casts three Jews who faithfully refuse to worship the work of any human hands. And God, the lonely one, in a gesture of scandalous and indefensible loyalty to his particular people, turns up in the furnace and preserves their lives.

Yet these lunges toward destruction, and miraculous stutter-steps back, are only the faintest preparation for the climax of the Gospels. Jesus has suffered death on the cross after a sham legal process, a death foreshadowed from the beginning of his story. Shocked and despondent as his followers must have been, their history, their lore, and the daily reality of being a subject people, in yet another idol-worshiping empire that didn't play games with difficult groups, had prepared them for this disappointment.

At this moment, early in the morning on the first day of the week, the day of Creation, Salome, Mary Magdalene, and Mary, the mother of James, go to Jesus's grave to anoint his body. They had stayed and watched while the men in their group had betrayed, denied, or fled in the critical hour. They had heard Jesus forgive those who punished him and promise Paradise to one who died next to him. They had watched some soldiers playing dice for his clothes and one insisting, at the last, that Jesus was innocent. Having seen all this, they come to fulfill their last measure of devotion, the honor that dust and earth give to each other.

There's nothing special about it. We've been doing it for ages. Their tears are perhaps more bitter than most, bitterness measuring their lost hope. But it's just another part of life. The love we show the vacant earth our friends leave behind and the care with which we tend it are beautiful. Mourning is nobility in defeat. Yes, all the clay will slip back into the river someday, and God will be lonely again, lonelier than at the first, lonelier than we are now, but until then we will have done our best. Like a mother brooding over her baby, the women will thrust their hands into the soft ointment and prepare Jesus for his long home. All they need is the spices and someone to help them roll away the stone.

The cross and suffering of Jesus, and the futile tenderness of his friends, stand in sharp contrast to our speculations about divine Providence. The cross places itself between the world's suffering and the pious refrain that "God has a plan," that God is above and outside it all in transcendent power. Somewhere in the smooth surface of those ideas a crack has to be found to stash the bodies, to give them a place in an otherwise orderly universe, to explain why the *something* that exists has to hurt.

Perhaps James Weldon Johnson was, like Mary, Mary, and Salome, finding something essential in the story. Perhaps the suffering reveals the true Providence, the hidden plan. Never was God lonelier than on the cross and in the tomb, yet humanity appears at God's side.

Hidden in Suffering

This seventh and last holy possession is the hardest to bear and the easiest to evade. The others are practices that people can enact. People may open the Word and hear it, baptize, share the holy meal, forgive sins, appoint leaders, and sing praises. By these things they can be visible to the world as Christians. The suffering of the cross, on the other hand, can only be imposed. Yet it is, in the words of theologian Vítor Westhelle, "the decisive material criterion" of the church. Without it, there is no true church.[3] More than anything else, it is what makes the Christian people dangerous in the world.

Christians, according to Luther, have to endure "every misfortune and persecution," whether "inward sadness, timidity, fear" or "outward poverty, contempt, illness, and weakness," because they wish to cling to Christ and because they are becoming like Christ. "They must be pious, quiet, obedient, and prepared to serve the government and everybody with life and goods, doing no one any harm," yet must endure "bitter hate." Indeed, so condemned must true Christians be, as heretics and "the most pernicious people on earth," that "those who hang, drown, murder, torture, banish, and plague them to death are," in the perverse but seemingly virtuous understanding of the fallen world, "rendering God a service."[4]

The image of the cross and the theme of suffering are woven through Christianity from the start. Jesus tells his followers that they will be rejected by family and killed by rulers, and that they should take up their crosses and follow him. The idea that good Christians ought to suffer, for their sins or the sins of the world, and to bear it in a saintly fashion was, in Luther's time, not very controversial. It remains common today. This idea has led some of Christianity's fiercest critics to conclude, not unreasonably, that Christians luxuriate in death and deprivation, blessing not the poor but poverty itself, worshiping not the Crucified One but crucifixion.

But for Luther, the cross goes deeper than our attitude toward suffering—into the very heart of how we know God. "He who does not know Christ does not know God hidden in suffering," he insists, since "God can be found *only* in suffering and the cross."[5] Because sin makes it impossible for us to perceive God directly in the creation and preservation of a good world, God chooses to reveal Godself to us in Christ crucified.

If you don't look for God in God's perfect essence, but instead find God revealed under "contrary signs," you are, in Luther's phrase, a "theologian of the cross." God's works are wisdom and power, but sin makes us incapable of seeing wisdom and always prone to abusing power. So God graciously embraced their opposites in order to become visible to faith.

If you don't look for God in God's perfect essence, but instead find God revealed under "contrary signs," you are, in Luther's phrase, a "theologian of the cross." God's works are wisdom and power, but sin makes us incapable of seeing wisdom and always prone to abusing power. So God graciously embraced their opposites in order to become visible to faith.

By contrast, what Luther called the "theologian of glory" looks on the invisible, eternal nature of God as if it were revealed to reason; this theologian therefore "prefers works to suffering, glory to the cross, strength to weakness, wisdom to folly, and, in general, good to evil."[6]

The idea of grasping God under contrary signs echoes Paul the Apostle, who called Christ crucified "folly" and "weakness."[7] And many ancient Christian writers emphasized the reversals enacted by a humiliated, crucified God. But what Luther sharpened to a knife-point is the idea that we know Christ crucified first, and only then God the Father. We know this redeeming death first, and only having seen this can we understand the world of nature, with all its fragmented beauty and its fleeting order, as Creation. Only after seeing our own attempts at goodness and righteousness condemned by the final emptying and absurdity of the cross can we know what it would mean to do a truly good work. Only having known God concealed in suffering can we hope to see God unveiled in glory.

As it is with God, so it is with the church: we grasp it under a contrary sign. The church does not judge the world, but is judged by it; it does not mount up in strength and beauty but languishes in weakness and privation; it does not glory in manifest good works but confesses its sin. It does not rest serene in God's invisible but certain omnipotence. Rather, the church comes in mourning to God's grave, and waits to be revealed with Christ in his resurrection.

So, as Luther put it, "The cross alone is our theology."[8] And when we make the cross central to our understanding of God and the church, we recover its political meaning. In the Roman

Empire, crucifixion was a penalty reserved for non-citizens. Rome used it to suppress rebellions and ensure order. It was an asphyxiating horror for the condemned and a threat to the survivors. So it mattered that Jesus died not by assassination or stoning or a fever. He died as a subjected and oppressed person, a criminal, and an example of humiliation to terrify others. So it was to be with Christians, whose public branding, killing, and banishment would be imposed and accomplished as a service to God.

The irony of the cross—its inversion of the world's values—is total and unconditional. "To say that the lowest can be the vessel of the highest is not a strong enough statement," Westhelle insists. "It would be more correct to say that only the lowest can encompass the highest; only the last can be the first; only the lost can be found."[9] Christ places his body between the weapons of oppression and the people they afflict.

The holy possession of the cross, which we honor in songs and paintings and in sculpture at the heart of our sanctuaries, throws a harsh light on the church. Our beautiful art, our heroic buildings, and our notable virtues point, subtly but unavoidably, to an unappeased absence. It is safer to make the cross into a capstone—the thing we have that other religions miss, the sin-canceling cherry on top of a good, rational, providential order visible to everyone.

Yet for all the ways we've decorated or hidden it, there it still is, an instrument of shameful, miserable death, present and insistent in all that we do as Christians. It is explicit and implicit in the lacerating confrontations of the Word. It humbles worldly status and distinction in the flood of baptism. It hovers over the mysterious democracy of the meal and the forgiveness of sins. It is present in the ministry pioneered by wobbly, crucified old Peter and in the pure contradiction of praise and thanksgiving amid an unredeemed world. To be conformed to the image of Christ in this world is to be conformed to the image of one who died as a forsaken outsider. On Easter morning, the only church visible in the world was three women preparing to anoint a corpse, at the risk of meeting the same fate.

Down by the Cross

The cross on which Jesus died was a brutal tool of civil inequality. And ever since, it's been impossible to encounter it as a sign of God's presence without encountering the world's continuing enactment of inequality. The cross casts the privileged and powerful down from their thrones, because they can't see the cross for what it is; it lifts up the lowly, because they know the cross from their own experience.

For most European and North American Christians, the experience of the cross is so distant as to be unreal. We cherish our martyrs, from Roman times down to anti-Nazi resisters Dietrich Bonhoeffer and Sophie Scholl. But it's easy to make them into the rule rather than the exception, and to focus on their lonely witness rather than the cooperation of whole Christian societies in the crimes those few resisted. It's easy to borrow their garb to cover the exaggerated feelings of persecution some of us experience today.

For many Christian churches, the experience of the cross survived only in the crosses we imposed on others. We periodically persecuted Jews and burned all copies of the Jewish Talmud we could find, sometimes mimicking an actual execution. Heretical Christians could meet a similar fate. Our churches dealt harshly with peasants and women who transgressed the political and religious order. And, eventually, we imposed the cross on the people we colonized and subjugated. In this ironic way, European Christians kept the theology of the cross alive in the experiences of the people we oppressed.

The twentieth-century American writer James Baldwin captured this irony of Christianity: "I am called Baldwin," he wrote, "because I was either sold by my African tribe or kidnapped out of it into the hands of a white Christian named Baldwin, who forced me to kneel at the foot of the cross."[10] In his youth he was a gifted preacher, and despite drifting from Christianity—or perhaps because he drifted from it—he never lost the profound scriptural and hymnic sensibility of the African-American church. "There is still, for me, no pathos quite like the pathos of those multicolored, worn, somehow triumphant and transfigured faces," he wrote, "speaking from the depths of a visible, tangible, continuing despair of the continuing goodness of the Lord."[11]

Yet in the world of white American and European Christianity, Baldwin could only see himself, and be seen, as an outsider. Staying in a tiny town in Alpine Switzerland where he was the first and only black visitor, he recalls the joy with which the bistro owner's wife explained to him that six Africans had been "bought" for baptism and salvation with the town's gifts. Her joy recalls him to his preacher father, "who, having taken his own conversion too literally, never, at bottom, forgave the white world (which he described as heathen) for having saddled him with a Christ in whom, to judge at least from their treatment of him, they themselves no longer believed."[12]

The faith that white Christians took so much pride in looked, to Baldwin, like hypocrisy or outright fraud. From his outsider's perspective, he could see things in a monument of their faith like the cathedral at Chartres that they could not see themselves:

> Perhaps they are struck by the power of the spires, the glory of the windows; but they have known God, after all, longer than I have known him, and in a different way, and I am terrified by the slippery bottomless well to be found in the crypt, down which heretics were hurled to death, and by the obscene, inescapable gargoyles jutting out of the stone and seeming to say that God and the devil can never be divorced. I doubt that the

> villagers think of the devil when they face a cathedral because they have never been identified with the devil.[13]

In the gargoyles and the bottomless well that swallowed heretics Baldwin almost finds God under "contrary signs," drawing very close to the theology of the cross. Yet, for all his skepticism and critical insight, he still took the white world's claims—about Christ, his cross, and his people, three things never to be separated—at face value, as if his own church and its hymns and traditions were Christian in a secondhand sense. The African-American church, whatever its flaws, was as true as any church in a thousand years and truer than many, charged with the truth of that church that was no more than three women on their way to a tomb.

Baldwin's words rolled back with a bitter sting after the massacre of nine members of Mother Emanuel A.M.E., a historic African-American church in Charleston, South Carolina. A young white man, consumed by the hostility and paranoia of the online white supremacist world, had attended a Bible study there, then killed the participants in the hope of sparking a race war. The church welcomed him warmly and without suspicion, as many black churches have welcomed me and other white visitors, and as I have often seen predominantly white churches fail to do. This welcome was so surprising to him that he apparently almost didn't go through with his crime. For that unguarded, faithful kindness to be answered so viciously was a heartbreaking reminder of how innocently and dangerously a suffering Christ travels.

The Emanuel massacre punctuated a series of infamous and polarizing killings of unarmed black people. The names of the victims, so easily lost to the obliviousness or calumny of the world, became rallying cries; the circumstances of their deaths became symbols of the hostility and suspicion under which they lived and died. Trayvon was buying Skittles. Jordan was playing music in his car. John was leaning on a BB gun in a Walmart. Tamir was in a park, given barely an instant to drop his toy gun.

In the responses to these deaths, I heard reluctance from many of my fellow white Americans to grant the victims innocence. For their deaths to make sense, they had to somehow be merited. White Christians did not, by and large, seem to discern the cross in any of this. The dead were "no angels." Their deaths were perhaps unfortunate, but no absurd offense to cosmic justice, the tearful vigils of their mothers no holy mourning at the tomb.

The victims at Mother Emanuel were different. White America could acknowledge their innocence. Their deaths, in a church, over Bibles, were indisputably a horror and an offense. They ministered the church, administered the library, educated the young. They were respectable. They were Christians. Unlike the killers of so many other unarmed black victims, their killer won no empathy and no crowd-funded legal defense. The astonishing grace of the families and survivors who extended forgiveness to the killer was received as a gesture of reconciliation writ large. The horror was quickly assimilated to our culture of mandatory uplift. It was an irresistible target for the theology of glory.

It wasn't difficult to ignore or obscure the cross of oppression in the midst of it. Eager as so many white Americans were to see the massacre as an aberration, as a spastic outburst from the margin, it was also a continuation of an old, evil history. During slavery, some of Emanuel's members were hanged for planning a slave revolt, and the church itself was razed to the ground. The pillars of the community who were slain were exactly the kinds of citizens who historically drew hostile notice and threats from a white world intent on keeping African-Americans in a narrowly defined place. The outrageous hostility of the killer was nothing new, but as old as the first Jamestown slave sale, as widespread as the federal housing policies designed to segregate cities, and as current as the modern incarceration state. His crime was no more arbitrary, and no less political, than the lynchings that gripped America for almost a century—celebratory communal spectacles that claimed more lives than three centuries of Roman persecution of Christians.[14]

All of these victims were sacred, testifying to the holiness of the cross and the suffering of Christ. God has always been hidden in the suffering of the people whose church resisted persecution and preserved its worshipers' humanity in a world that sought ever to deny it. This church—James Baldwin's church—appropriated the Exodus and the dispossession of Ruth and the rebuilding of Jerusalem as its own story. While European Christians sang, to Jesus, "I, it was, denied thee / I crucified thee," this church agreed, from a different perspective: "See how they done my Lord."

When we encounter the fact of oppression, we can choose to enter deeply and unreservedly into the reality of suffering and our role in creating it. Or we can choose to flee the fear and anxiety this suffering provokes for the safety of a shallow and premature resolution. Just as we can choose whether to embrace or escape the staggering economy of the Word, the infinite obligation in the water, and the stringent intimacy of the meal, we can embrace the cross or seek glory instead.

When we encounter the fact of oppression, we can choose to enter deeply and unreservedly into the reality of suffering and our role in creating it. Or we can choose to flee the fear and anxiety this suffering provokes for the safety of a shallow and premature resolution.

Contrary Signs

Whether we want it or not, whether we embrace it, flee it, or try somehow to do both, the cross is at the heart of the church's presence in the world, and at the heart of its politics. The cross interprets and judges our most noble "social ministry" and our most virtuous public positions. It asks, "Does this embrace the God revealed in suffering and shame, or does it deny that God for the sake of something else?"

As long as the cross stands in sanctuaries, its question cannot be avoided. Yet, escaping suffering is the great preoccupation of our age. Our politics and our economic ideology promise to help us if we do our part. Hard work and good habits can nudge us ahead of our demographic destiny. With greater success we can use the subdivision and the school district boundary to cut ourselves off from the world's troubles. Those who get to the very top can buy an estate in New Zealand to flee to should climate change or state failure swamp even the prosperous suburb.

It is only responsible to try to do this, to take whatever avenues of escape are available to us. Our world promises that, with enough ingenuity and raw power, not all of us have to end up in the same muddy riverbed from which we were formed.

The cross, and the people who possess it, bear witness to a different promise and a different responsibility.

There was a special shock and shudder in the revelation that the killer at Mother Emanuel was baptized, raised, and confirmed in a church in my denomination, the Evangelical Lutheran Church in America. We are a virtuous church. We strive to be open and welcoming. Until this horrific event, it had been possible to find a small, consoling margin of difference between *us* and whatever *them* was a little more responsible for a particular crime or injustice, despite the fact that the ELCA is one of the very whitest churches in America. I couldn't stop thinking of that church and its people, people surely much like those I serve with.

At the same time, two of the Charleston victims were educated in a seminary of our church. They were part of our family, too, not just as fellow Christians but as people who had shared the Word and reflected on all the holy possessions of Christian life alongside those who would serve those overwhelmingly white churches. And they had left Emanuel open and welcoming to one of us who intended monstrous evil to them.

Not two weeks after the massacre, the scheduled readings for worship gave us the Lamentations of Jeremiah:

> It is good for one to bear
>   the yoke in youth,
> to sit alone in silence
>   when the LORD has imposed it,
> to put one's mouth to the dust
>   (there may yet be hope),
> to give one's cheek to the smiter,
>   and be filled with insults. (3:27-30)

We heard the story of a woman with a twelve-year hemorrhage touching the garment of Jesus and being healed, and the story of Jesus raising a child from the dead. Such words sound different, do different things, and point to the cross in different ways for different people. Some are allowed to smite and insult while others must bear it. Some have their mouths pushed to the dust, and others must kiss the dust in repentance. Some have bled for too long, and some learn too late that their own hearts must bleed too.

Last and First

The wonder—an offensive, scandalous wonder—of the body of Christ is that it contains both groups. It contains those who have to fight each day to preserve their own humanity, and those who learn to their shock that they have not yet achieved their humanity while their brothers and sisters are oppressed. It contains opposite sorrows and opposite consolations, gravitating toward and radiating from that Roman cross. This is more than empathy; it is the naming of an unbreakable bond between those who with divine strength forgive a resonant evil and those who must ask forgiveness. As it was at that first moment of crucifixion, so it continues to be. The people gathered around Christ included those who stayed and those who fled, who defended and denied, who betrayed and pleaded, who played dice and proclaimed innocence, and one who died with Christ's blessing on the same day.

So long as the cross is there, it demands and proclaims an unconditional, essential identification of the church with the oppressed, the despised, and the suffering. Should their lot—our lot—be amended by some new or revised social or economic order, new classes to despise will take their place. Race is a creation of history, after all; if we were to move beyond our present categories, we would be more than capable of creating new ones. Physical ability, age, stage of development, skin hue, genitalia, mental health or cognitive capacity, sexuality, economic function, financial status, religion—any of them will serve the purpose, have served the purpose. Spires will always need their gargoyles.

> So long as the cross is there, it demands and proclaims an unconditional, essential identification of the church with the oppressed, the despised, and the suffering.

That is why this holy possession of the cross, more than all the rest, is a dagger pointed at the heart of our world's illusions—whether of safety, power, sanctity, or justice. It can never be halfway reconciled to innocent suffering by our politicians and preachers, but rather vindicates the ones who suffer. It can never tolerate the insidious rationalizations for sacrificing a piece of God's handiwork for some urgent human purpose, but proclaims the treasure of each life. It can never accept our bereaving of God, or his lonely, maternal tears, over these lumps of clay. It will not leave any death unconsoled; it will not leave any tear undried; it will not deprive the dehydrated, asphyxiated Christ of his claim over every suffering thing.

It was their willingness to encounter suffering without mitigation or hope that brought those women to the tomb on the first day when so many others ran the other way. And there, because they already possessed the cross, they encountered the first truly new thing since that other first day. Because they possessed the cross, and knew its suffering, they came to the one corner of the earth where its power had been broken, and where the Empire and the world itself had come to an end.

Conclusion: The Space Between

Whenever we look at a religion through its central practices, we can't help but be struck by contrasts. We see the contrast between the ritual and the story that explains it, between the reality and the ideal, between the present and the history that leads to it.

This is most certainly true when we look at Christianity and its holiest possessions. Each of these possessions highlights contrasts: between the world as it is and the world as it appears in the words, water, and wine; between the faith that fervently believes everything these possessions convey and the doubt that hedges on their fulfillment; between the wild end-times ethic they embody and the stubborn ordinariness of the people who hold them. These contrasts don't divide one kind of Christian from another, or even Christians from non-Christians. They are visible everywhere, to everyone.

These contrasts can be awkward and painful. They push those who experience them toward a resolution, one way or another. Worship should be more realistic or else more otherworldly. Faith should be shrunk to our capacity to believe, or doubt should be stigmatized and excluded. The church should be more pure and homogenous, or the wild ethic should be bargained down to the price we can pay.

But this gap between God's kingdom and the kingdoms of this world, between faith and doubt, between ideals and reality—this is exactly the space these signs direct us to. It's where the holy possessions live and do their work. This gap is where all the action is. In the space between, possibilities have the chance to become plausible. Childish dreams can become hard-tested hopes.

These signs do not require belief, because they defer the question of belief and rejection. They are unaccustomed; they break life's rhythm; they reconfigure the world whether we assent to it or not. Like a pebble in a shoe, they can change our minds by their mere presence.

A paradox lies at the heart of all these practices: only for the sake of doubt do we need them, but only for the sake of faith do they build us up. There is a way that faith formation is supposed to go in liturgy and theology. We come first as inquirers and observers. We listen and learn. We adopt a worldview, a conviction, an identity that is deepened and made real by the sacraments.

But it doesn't necessarily work that way. Worldviews are fragile. They are fraught with contradictions and weak points that can be exploited with devastating effect. The smallest hole of doubt—about whether all the animals could have fit on that ark, for instance—is sufficient to unravel an entire "biblical worldview."

These possessions are harder habits to acquire, more fragmentary to assemble, less impressive to look at, perhaps even less persuasive as guides. But they are more durable. Our doctrines and worldviews were mostly built to defend and make sense of them. They allow for the truth that we move between faith and doubt, commitment and lassitude. The mind will wander, but the body feels the sting of wine and the movement of pardon. The body will falter, but a word calls it back.

These possessions are harder habits to acquire, more fragmentary to assemble, less impressive to look at, perhaps even less persuasive as guides. But they are more durable.

These signs can guide us without requiring a systematic program of reform, a transcendence of Christian divisions, or a perfect rejoinder to the criticisms leveled by the ideologues of a secular age. No old or new expression of Christianity is needed to do these things. They are simply there, as gifts for the whole church, and through the church to the whole world. That church is present and visible wherever these possessions are grasped, and whenever people follow their prompting. As Bonhoeffer wrote, the church is not an "ought" trying to become an "is." Where we already are, and what we already do, is the mystery. That these few practices can take place, and even take root, among people of such variable faith, in such momentary and marginal events, is a profound witness to grace in a world that knows how to create an abundance of almost everything else.

Grace is where these possessions originate, and grace is where they ultimately lead in their spiraling itinerary of Christian life. They come, we profess, from a God we can at best perceive dimly, and more often not at all; a God who may live in our minds as no more than a name for a mystery and a possibility; a God who wishes more and higher and harder and better things for us than we would dare to ask or imagine. That's what grace is: excess of blessing over what we earn, of yearning over our power to know; of desire over our capacity to enjoy. Grace is the gift of words calling us to extravagant attentiveness, repentance, and generosity while the world cuts wisdom and prudence down to a useful size. Grace washes and unites people beyond all boundaries while the world vigorously defends those same boundaries. Grace names, condemns, and releases grave evils unconditionally and forever while the world hides, manages, and indulges them for the sake of peace and prosperity. Grace calls and consecrates people to lead by mere service and blessing while the world cultivates subtle and even unknowing agents of domination. Grace transforms work into the solemn leisure of praise and thanksgiving while the world toils for fragile gain. Grace endures suffering, transforming it by love into resurrection, while the world imposes the cross and flees its victims.

In these brutally ordinary things, we encounter grace as the fundamental fact of existence. They are not mysterious additions to a clear and visible universe, but a hard-as-nails foundation for experiencing the universe's fathomless mysteries. Each of us, let alone all of us together, is so improbable as to be effectively impossible—our universe stabilizing a hair's breadth from chaos, our genes and circumstances combining in ludicrous contingency. All of us together, let alone each of us individually, are so small in this universe that we can hardly be said to exist at all, just a momentary convergence of matter and energy that will dissipate in infinite directions before any other intelligent life in the universe will be likely to notice us. "The eternal silence of these infinite spaces frightens me," French philosopher Blaise Pascal said, as humans were barely starting to get a sense of the size of those spaces.[1] Like so many religious neurotics, he was merely ahead of his time. In space, in time, in probability, we all disappear. The rest, before and after, is silence.

In these mere undeniable facts of words spoken, water poured, and forgiveness proclaimed, grace gives this silent world back to us. But in these things, the world comes not as a problem to solve but as a gift. Your momentary concentration of fourteen-billion-year-old particles, your voice's tiny vibration, and your capacity to be made a sister of a stranger are your impress upon a sullen universe. They are the blunt facts that reveal the miracle. "Although the miracles of the visible world of nature have lost their value for us because we see them continually," Augustine wrote, "still, if we observe them wisely, they will be found to be greater miracles than the most extraordinary and unusual events."[2]

These possessions reveal the order we create within this wild universe to be much more fragile and precious and vicious than we know. Even at its best—our best—this order courts its own destruction. Nebuchadnezzar built a great idol and called it religious unity. Rome made a desert and called it peace. Modern capitalism creates massive inequality and calls it prosperity. And those goods—the unity, the peace, the prosperity—are real, even when we acknowledge, as we sometimes must, that the unity comes at the cost of a fiery furnace, the peace at the cost of crucifixion, the prosperity at the cost of the occasional word-shattering crisis. Those goods are real, even when we acknowledge that this whole enterprise of civilization is temporary, that the sand in the hourglass only runs one way.

History, W. H. Auden once wrote, "is predictable in the degree to which all men love themselves, and spontaneous in the degree to which each man loves God and through Him his neighbor."[3] These sacred signposts, and the people who follow them, are a vector of unpredictability in this world. They create an unwalled city, porous to the stranger, misfit, and newcomer from without, and from within to the world-changing improvisatory power of people who mimic drowning, drink divine blood, and pronounce pardon from eternity. It is not necessary that these possessions be practiced with the utmost clarity, or that the people who practice them embody their untamed grace everywhere and always. We will still make peace with the world's faults, try to find a corner of the world to stand on, agree to give the devil his due and no more. It is only necessary that these signs endure. They make the body of Christ stand out in the world—for mockery, admiration, or puzzlement; they draw the outsider inward and push the insider outward at the same time, inevitably, whether anyone wishes it or not. The more they are held, practiced, and cherished, the sharper the contrast they will make, and the heavier the traffic will be, in both directions, across that body's porous edge. By enduring, they will resist the world. By enduring, they will make explicit the love from which all things come and to which they will all resolve.

They make the body of Christ stand out in the world—for mockery, admiration, or puzzlement; they draw the outsider inward and push the insider outward at the same time, inevitably, whether anyone wishes it or not.

It isn't even necessary that the people gathered around these possessions be vast in number. Christians in the world may be, as our ancient texts say, like the salt of the earth, the yeast in the dough, the soul in the body, the alien city of God on pilgrimage; they may be in the world but not of it, of no account in themselves but giving life to the whole.[4] Christians may be, as the Scriptures often suggest, a remnant. A remnant is scattered, fragile, utterly dependent on God. A remnant survives in dispersed outcasts, or in those dozen disciples foolish enough to linger after Jesus tells them they must eat his flesh and drink his blood, or even in three women coming to a tomb at dawn.[5]

It is a grave thought that a child baptized today may prove to be one of the few threads connecting the Christians of today to whoever we are in years to come. Or that someone happening upon church on a Sunday will prove to be the random patch of good soil on which the words fussed over and despaired of on a Saturday night will fall. Or that someone will be suddenly shocked and secretly nourished by bread broken and wine poured, and will seek them out and strive to share them ever after.

But if the Christian people are, and will be, a remnant, it will not be merely a *saved* remnant but also a *saving* remnant. Together, these possessions and the people who share them will point beyond the limits of the world that rations mercy and does not know grace and hoards what must, and will, ultimately be released.

In these actions we take together, everyone who comes must have the chance to hear, everyone who wishes to become a brother or sister must be made one, everyone who hungers must be fed, everyone who asks, to them it must be given. People who break bread together at the command of Christ really do become, if only in that instant, one body, his body, in the world. And in the world that is coming, every word, every washing in the water, every meal and act of forgiveness and song of praise and vigil at the tomb will make the world shudder. They will be what they always have been: the defiant rejoicing of a community gathered around a crucified God. They will reach past everything we frantically make and protect to that kingdom where the least blessing is purely a gift. They will make that kingdom real among the scattered and motley crowd that grasps them, here and there, in streets and suburbs and refugee camps, as they are conformed to the image of Christ in the world. And they will make that kingdom real to the incredulous world that watches. May grace come.

Acknowledgments

When you write compulsively, the notion of writing a book comes naturally. Everything beyond the notion comes a lot harder. I owe many thanks to Lil Copan for helping me formulate this book and for editing it so vigorously and carefully. I'm grateful to the friends who took time to read the chapters and push me to make them better in countless ways: Theodor Dunkelgrün, John Flack, Elizabeth Palmer, Amy Ziettlow, Katy Scrogin, Jason Hines, Daniel Schultz, Erin Bouman, and Bromleigh McCleneghan.

Many different editors helped plant the seeds of this book in dozens of different articles. I am particularly grateful to John Gravois, Steve Thorngate, Ed Lake, Charles Petersen, Kolby Yarnell, Evan Derkacz, Lisa Webster, and Brook Wilensky-Lanford.

The people of many churches received me as a preacher and pastor, helping me to learn almost everything I can claim to know about holding and practicing our faith in a secular world and inspiring me to share it in this way. Thanks in particular to Luther Memorial Church, Wicker Park Lutheran Church, Bethel-Imani Lutheran Church, all in Chicago; to St. Mark's Lutheran Church in Aurora; and to the unendingly patient and kind people of Messiah Lutheran Church in Wauconda, Illinois. Thank you to Augustana Lutheran Church and Lutheran Campus Ministry for re-introducing me to Christ at the right time, and to the numerous clergy mentors who guided me, especially Nancy Goede, John Gorder, Susan Swanson, Ray Legania, Linda Packard, Cynthia Lindner, Frank Senn, and the late Ruth VanDemark. And deep thanks to Dawn Mass Eck for being such a supportive and endlessly patient colleague throughout this process.

I am grateful to Mary Hietbrink, Rachel Brewer, and everyone else at Eerdmans who helped make this book first possible, and then better.

Finally, I confess the humblest possible debt to that great academy of theologians who wrote by night after their duties as pastors, bishops, and abbots were attended to and the task of reflection was finally open to them. Their striving to illuminate the faith by which they lived and worked has inspired my own modest attempts to write from the midst of the Christian community. If all my writing accomplishes is to lead readers to Augustine, Luther, Bonhoeffer, and many others not directly quoted here, I will count it a success.

Notes

Notes to Chapter 1

1. "Word" in Christianity is a term used in several different and important ways. It refers, in the first instance, to the Second Person of the Trinity, the *logos* of God the Father. It can also refer to the divine speech acts recorded in the Scriptures, to the messages brought from God by the prophets and apostles, and finally to the text of the Bible itself. Luther tended to speak of the Word in the sense of divine speech and human oral proclamation, with the written New Testament existing only as an unfortunate necessity (see *Luther's Works*, vol. 52: *Sermons II*, ed. Hans J. Hillerbrand and Helmut T. Lehmann [Philadelphia: Fortress Press, 1974], pp. 205–6). According to Luther, the Word of God in Scripture, in preaching, and in pastoral acts like confession and forgiveness is what "conveys Christ." The written Scriptures are a necessary witness and repository of the Word itself. So I have in some cases referred to the Bible as the Word in a rhetorical sense, as the part for the whole.

2. Quoted in Lawrence W. Levine, *Black Culture and Black Consciousness: Afro-American Folk Thought from Slavery to Freedom* (Oxford: Oxford University Press, 2007), p. 47.

3. Søren Kierkegaard, *Fear and Trembling*, trans. Alastair Hannay (London: Penguin, 1985), p. 100.

4. St. Augustine, *The City of God*, trans. Henry Bettenson (London: Penguin, 1972), X.14, p. 392.

5. The line is from a lost treatise, quoted by Augustine in *City of God*, VII.11, p. 251.

6. *Luther's Works*, vol. 41: *Church and Ministry III*, ed. Eric W. Gritsch (Philadelphia: Fortress Press, 1966), p. 149.

Notes to Chapter 2

1. *Luther's Works,* vol. 41: *Church and Ministry III,* ed. Eric W. Gritsch (Philadelphia: Fortress Press, 1966), p. 151.

2. *Didache* 4:8.

3. 1 Peter 2:9–10.

4. *Letter to Diognetus* 5:1–4.

5. *Martin Luther: Selections from His Writings,* ed. John Dillenberger (New York: Anchor, 1962), p. 292.

6. *Martin Luther: Selections from His Writings,* p. 302.

7. Gianni Valene, "Pope Francis: To evangelize baptism is enough," *La Stampa,* April 18, 2013, http://www.lastampa.it/2013/04/18/vaticaninsider/eng/the-vatican/pope-francis-to-evangelize-baptism-is-enough-FXyXo-Hth3EMzFgqwy4ZilO/pagina.html. Accessed August 23, 2016.

8. St. Augustine, *The City of God,* trans. Henry Bettenson (London: Penguin, 1972), XIX.17, p. 878.

Notes to Chapter 3

1. The discussion here is indebted to Paul F. Bradshaw, *Eucharistic Origins* (Eugene, OR: Wipf & Stock, 2012).

2. "Confession Concerning Christ's Supper," in *Luther's Works,* vol. 37: *Word and Sacrament III,* trans. and ed. Robert H. Fischer (Philadelphia: Fortress Press, 1961), p. 219.

3. "Confession Concerning Christ's Supper," p. 217.

4. "Confession Concerning Christ's Supper," p. 224.

5. Sara Miles, *Take This Bread* (New York: Ballantine, 2007), p. 59.

6. Thomas O'Loughlin, *The Didache: A Window on the Earliest Christians* (Grand Rapids: Baker Academic, 2010), p. 104.

Notes to Chapter 4

1. St. Augustine, *The City of God,* trans. Henry Bettenson (London: Penguin, 1972), XIV.15, p. 575.

2. John Britton, "Death, Disease, and Tobacco," *The Lancet,* April 5, 2017.

3. *Luther's Works,* vol. 41: *Church and Ministry III: Liturgy and Hymns,* ed. Eric W. Gritsch (Philadelphia: Fortress Press, 1966), p. 153.

4. St. Augustine, *The City of God,* XIV.14, p. 574.

5. *Luther's Works,* vol. 1: *Lectures on Genesis, Chapters 1–5,* ed. Jaroslav Pelikan (Saint Louis: Concordia, 1958), p. 105.

6. Large Catechism, in *The Book of Concord,* ed. Robert Kolb and Timothy J. Wengert (Minneapolis: Fortress Press, 2000), p. 478.

7. Frank C. Senn, *Christian Liturgy: Catholic and Evangelical* (Minneapolis: Fortress Press, 1997), pp. 155–56, 197.

8. Fyodor Dostoyevsky, *The Brothers Karamazov,* trans. Constance Garnett (New York: Penguin, 1957), p. 239.

9. Dietrich Bonhoeffer, *Life Together,* trans. John W. Doberstein (New York: Harper & Row, 1954), pp. 112–13. I have not altered the gendered language of the translation, trusting the assumption that it applies equally to men and women.

10. "Smalcald Articles," in *The Book of Concord,* ed. Robert Kolb and Timothy J. Wengert (Minneapolis: Fortress Press, 2000), p. 313.

Notes to Chapter 5

1. *Luther's Works,* vol. 41: *Church and Ministry III,* ed. Eric W. Gritsch (Philadelphia: Fortress Press, 1966), p. 154.

2. Dietrich Bonhoeffer, *Life Together,* trans. John W. Doberstein (New York: Harper & Row, 1954), p. 108.

3. For example in his Holy Thursday homily, 2013 (https://w2.vatican.va/content/francesco/en/homilies/2013/documents/papa-francesco_20130328_messa-crismale.html. Accessed August 30, 2016.

Notes to Chapter 6

1. Marilynne Robinson, *Lila* (New York: Farrar, Straus & Giroux, 2014), p. 74.

2. *Luther's Works,* vol. 41: *Church and Ministry III,* ed. Eric W. Gritsch (Philadelphia: Fortress Press, 1966), p. 164.

3. Hosea 14:2 (NRSV), note p.

4. *Didache* 10.6.

5. Pseudo-Dionysius, *The Complete Works,* trans. Colm Luibheid (Mahwah, NJ: Paulist Press, 1987), pp. 68–69.

6. See Thomas Aquinas, *Summa Theologica,* II IIe q83a6.

7. *The Book of Concord: The Confessions of the Evangelical Lutheran*

Church, ed. Robert Kolb and Timothy Wengert (Minneapolis: Fortress Press, 2000), p. 356.

8. St. Augustine, *Confessions*, trans. R. S. Pine-Coffin (London: Penguin, 2003), I.5, p. 5.

9. Andrew Newborn and Mark Robert Waldman, *How God Changes Your Brain* (New York: Random House, 2009).

10. Walter Brueggemann, *Sabbath as Resistance* (Louisville: Westminster John Knox Press, 2014), p. vi.

Notes to Chapter 7

1. *Luther's Works*, vol. 41: *Church and Ministry III: Liturgy and Hymns*, ed. Eric W. Gritsch (Philadelphia: Fortress Press, 1966), pp. 164–65.

2. James Weldon Johnson, "The Creation," in *The Norton Anthology of African-American Literature*, ed. Henry L. Gates and Nellie McKay (New York: W. W. Norton, 1997), pp. 775–77.

3. Vítor Westhelle, *The Church Event: The Call and Challenge of the Church Protestant* (Minneapolis: Augsburg Fortress Press, 2009), p. 86.

4. *Luther's Works*, vol. 41, p. 165.

5. "Theses for the Heidelberg Disputation," in Timothy F. Lull, ed., *Martin Luther's Basic Theological Works* (Minneapolis: Fortress Press, 1989), p. 44 (emphasis added).

6. "Theses for the Heidelberg Disputation," pp. 43–44.

7. See 1 Corinthians 1:18–31.

8. Quoted in Vítor Westhelle, *The Scandalous God: The Use and Abuse of the Cross* (Minneapolis: Fortress Press, 2006), p. 110.

9. "Theses for the Heidelberg Disputation," p. 25.

10. James Baldwin, *Collected Essays* (New York: Library of America, 1998), p. 335.

11. Baldwin, *Collected Essays*, p. 306.

12. James Baldwin, *Notes of a Native Son* (Boston: Beacon Press, 1955), p. 163.

13. Baldwin, *Notes of a Native Son*, p. 174.

14. For an excellent account of theological reactions (or lack thereof) to lynching in America, see James Cone, *The Cross and the Lynching Tree* (Maryknoll, NY: Orbis Books, 2011).

Notes to the Conclusion

1. Blaise Pascal, *Pensées*, trans. W. F. Trotter (New York: Dutton, 1958), Pensée no. 206 (p. 61).

2. St. Augustine, *The City of God*, trans. Henry Bettenson (London: Penguin, 1972), X.12, p. 390.

3. W. H. Auden, *Collected Poems* (New York: Random House, 1991), p. 388.

4. The *Epistle to Diognetus*, ch. 6.

5. See Isaiah 11:11–12; John 6:66–70; Mark 16:1–3.